The Drinking Man's Guide To Women (and Divorce)

By

Patrick O'Cahir

Argus Enterprises International, Inc
Book Publishers
North Carolina***New Jersey

The Drinking Man's Guide to
Understanding Divorce
All rights reserved © 2009
by Patrick O'Cahir

A-Argus Better Book Publishers, LLC

For information:
A-Argus Better Book Publishers, LLC
9001 Ridge Hill Drive
Kernersville, North Carolina 27284
www.a-argusbooks.com

ISBN: 978-0-6155322-8-8
ISBN: 0-6155322-8-4

Book Cover designed by Patrick O'Cahir

Printed in the United States of America

Foreword

The more I drank, the better she looked.

-John B. Daniels

Table of Contents

Foreword

This book is for men only. It bashes women. If you are not a man put the friggin' book back on the shelf.

The next 75,000 words may get you through one of the most difficult times of your life. It is designed to help you understand that your divorce was her fault-not yours. It details the differences between men and women. Take a minute to laugh at these differences. They exist for a reason. Since most divorces are sought by women- you are not alone. There are many support groups that may help. But who wants to air their dirty laundry with a bunch of whining strangers? Reading this acerbic drivel also gives you an excuse to drink alone for a couple of weeks and lick your wounds. So what? At least you don't have to drive home from a bar and risk a DUI.

Each chapter has suggestions for trying a new spirit and a new kind of beer. Do not try to read this book all at once! I suggest one chapter per night. First, being male, you do not have the attention span to attempt this feat. Second, you will be too plastered after each chapter to even turn the page.

So, get blitzed, but most of all, feel better that your divorce was not personal - it was biological. Like all women that file for divorce-she's just another self serving bitch.

Communication

Appetizer
One shot of Jim Beam Whiskey

Main Course
Molson Golden Ale

Men and women communicate differently. There is a reason for this behavior; one that has to do with the survival of the species or something like that. Who cares what the reason is? How many times have you had a discussion with your ex-wife and one of you says that the other is not listening? Or you walked away totally confused how she got *that* from what you said? If you have already downed your shot of whiskey, pop open a beer. Here we go.

Many years ago, someone came up with the idea that women were great communicators. Since that time, men have been portrayed as being out of touch with their thoughts and unable to adequately express how they feel. Anyone that has even a passing interest in history knows that may not be entirely accurate. Actually it is bull-crap. Men have historically been very effective communicators, while women are not as in touch with their feelings as they would like everyone to think.

For the last century, industrial women have attempted to describe themselves as emotionally complex creatures that are synched tightly with their mysterious, intricate thoughts. A fraction of women even commiserate that men are bumbling idiots with no clue as to what women need.

This misunderstanding has become the basis for the many failed relationships that exist today. These myths are perpetuated in our society by the mass media. But are they true?

Through Darwinian necessity, men have developed a complex communication system. The system evolved from the simple hand signals of cave dwellers up to present day satellites that can communicate instantaneously anywhere in the world. Women have remained in a conversational mode that is somewhat rudimentary. Does that mean one is better than the other? Is this a reason to look down your nose at your lovely ex-wife? Heck, no. It means that we are different and I am about to postulate a possible reason as to why. Drink your beer.

Let us go back 10,000 years ago, when humans existed as hunter-gathers in small communal societies. Who were the hunters? Men. Who were the gatherers? Women. We evolved in the same city but different streets. Same house but different rooms. Men hunted big game for the life-sustaining meat, laden with protein, fats and vitamins. Women stayed behind with the children and gathered berries, nuts and herbs. One may question why women did not go out and hunt while the men stayed back, but that would imply equality between the sexes at a biological level. The biology led to the culture. One look at our physiology tells us men and women are different. A three-year-old could figure that out. Ten thousand years of human cultural history reveal that men and women look, think, and act differently. Men and women *are* different. So it makes sense to say that we most likely communicate in different ways.

The men went hunting because they are genetically predisposed to hunt. Nature and/or God made them that way. Anyway, hunting is risky business. Men had to interact effectively to hunt; especially for big game like Woolly Mammoths. Getting one of those tusks stuck in you could wreck the whole trip. Communication was important for many reasons; most of which were based on pure survival. Successful hunters had to sneak up on the prey, kill it, carve it up before other animals attacked him, and bring the meat back to their clan. Men with spears that conveyed their intentions to other men with spears were more successful at pursuing and killing their quarry. These triumphant hunters brought the meat back and nourished their families. The men that communicated well had offspring that were well-fed and healthy. Non-communicative, dimwitted hunters scared away their targets. They did not coordinate their attack. These bumbling idiots went hungry. Their children ate infrequently and succumbed to either disease or predators. Or both. Nature selects for certain traits that are beneficial to a species survival. The trait of being an effective communicator was selected as one in human males. Good hunters signaled, and interpreted other's signals, through a complicated series of grunts, limb movement, head nods, eye cues, and body language. Communication skills were an advantageous trait from an early stage of our evolution. As society became more advanced, history shows that men adapted their communication skills to the new technologies.

Some men made marks on wood, bones, clay tablets, and eventually papyrus, to record and convey their most profound reflections to other men. The recipient of these inspirations could understand what was being expressed and respond back using the same marks. A bunch of guys in Phoenicia developed an alphabet around 3500 B.C. Around the same time, Sumerian men invented cuneiform writing; pictographs of accounts written on clay tablets. These fragments of intellect were forwarded to each successive generation. Some fellows painted their ideas on walls. The Age of the Written Word was dawning. The use of smoke signals allowed men to express their intentions over great distances. Communicating ideas became a male trait.

Ω

Meanwhile, women stayed back and raised the children. They waited for the men to return from the hunt- and later the expedition or the Crusade. They filled their hours with discussions. Those discussions centered around men because their men ensured the survival of the female and her offspring. To summarize succinctly, men and women learned to communicate in very different ways. Drink your beer.

Ω

Smoke signals, hand signals, facial expressions, arm movements, symbols written on paper, rock and wood. These became the domain of the human male of the species. Men would tell stories of the hunt. Women listened. (Most had no choice.) Gentlemen, we can be quite overwhelming as we brag about ourselves. It was around 776 B.C. when homing pigeons were first used to send messages, scrawled on bits of papyrus, across great distances. Homing pigeons. Little gray birds trained to carry tiny letters across the vast skies. It is overwhelming to intellectualize the magnanimity of such an endeavor, one animal training another to carry messages indecipherable, and incomprehensible, to the carrier. Yet, human males had successfully undertaken this advance in the exchange of ideas. There is no record to indicate that women ever used pigeons, or any other type of early transmission technology. From that pivotal point in history, men extensively recorded their thoughts in scrolls; eventually storing these scrolls in great libraries. The knowledge base became more than male bravado. It became history. It chronicled the adventures of individual men melded with narratives from the experiences and philosophies of other men. Men communicated thoughts beyond the simple intentions of a hunter about to throw his spear. It was the birth of civilization; signed, sealed and delivered by the communication skills of male human beings. Drink your beer and stop talking out loud while you're reading.

Before we get too far ahead here, let us not leave women in the Stone Age. What were women doing while men were developing these communication systems? From the early cave days, women were developing a communication system amongst themselves. Picking berries and caring for children did not lend the brain to the intellectual pressures necessary to leap forth and advance intricate communicative abilities. Women spoke, and gesticulated, mainly to each other while their men were away. What were the topics of discussion during those long days of gathering berries? Watch out for the unripe berries? There is a bug on my berry? Do not touch my berries? Women quickly bored of these discussions. There was no "pressure" for varied communication techniques to evolve. If a saber-toothed tiger appeared each women would save herself and her children. It was actually a survival advantage if the saber-toothed tiger filled his belly with another women or *her* children. Meow. Think about that for a minute. Survival as cave people had a lasting effect upon our collective psyches. (A sip of beer is optional here.)

Women also competed with each other for their share of the kill. As history progressed and men ventured out more and more, this "kill" could have been the booty from a war. Or the gold from a Crusade to the Middle East. When the men came back from their jaunt, each woman was given their share according to her husband's rank in the group. The alpha male received the most, as did his wife and children, and so on down the line. Sound familiar? In a scenario such as that, talking may not be a way of finding solutions, but of obtaining information. Could it be that women evolved a communication system that obtained as much information as they could on other women? Maybe even to the point of deceiving the other woman about her status? If a woman could convince the others that their husband was not worth appropriating would she not solidify her place in the clan? Is this why women spend a fair amount of time bashing their husbands and boyfriends? Has this behavior has carried forth into modern society? Consider the following conversation from 10,000 years ago. (I have taken the liberty to translate ancient cave dialect.)

Wilma: "Your husband always brings home a lot of meat."

Betty: "That may be true, but he never does anything with the kids. And he snores. Plus, he is always working on his spear..."

Wilma: " I hear ya, sister. Mine is always hanging out with his brother. They sewed some old skins into a ball and go out to the field to throw it back and forth. How boring."

Betty: "Where are all the good cavemen?"

Wilma: "Beats me."

Throughout the last 10,000 years men and women have developed a completely different communication system. Although men and women used the same language to obtain information, the interpretation was different. A man transferred information that assured his *immediate* survival and position in society. Women transferred information that assured her *long-term* survival and position in society. A man needed a quick answer. Was the deer behind the rock? Yes or no? Women needed to know that *their* dear would rock their world and provide for her and the children. Both systems work but are subject to misinterpretation by the opposite sex. You think I am full of shit? Huh? Ever try to solve a problem posed by your ex-wife?

The hapless husband, in his endeavor to solve his ex-wife's problems, is oblivious to one simple fact. She does not want a solution. She just wants to talk. Talking allows her to garner information and feel close to him. He thinks she wants a legitimate solution. What she wants is to get more mileage out of the problem so he will continue to talk to her. She wants to involve him in her world but does not know how. So she subconsciously perpetuates a problem. When hubby actually solves the problem, the conversation is over. Women like to talk. It soothes them. The last thing a woman wants is for the conversation to be over. Sorry to be so stark and frank on that one. Eventually, men get frustrated and make a decision. Decision-making ends the interaction. Maybe this is why decision-making is not a strength of human females. It was not naturally selected for over the course of our cultural evolution. Women tend to avoid making decisions by chatting endlessly about a situation. Unable to make clear decisions she becomes frustrated and lashes out at her husband. She pouts and complains. He will be punished subsequently by the "silent treatment", withholding of sexual favors or, my personal favorite, the classic slamming of the cabinet doors. This behavior continues until he kisses up to her and makes her feel safe again by cuddling and making cooing sounds. And talking. Women are calmed by this actions. The man leaves confused and bewildered at this irrational behavior. After all, she approached him with the problem. Sound familiar? Drink your beer before your blood pressure goes up.

This disparity in spoken language is part of the reason that women differ from men intellectually. They do not connect the dots the same way that men do. By nightfall in caveman time, the men were back at camp, describing (with embellishment) the story of the hunt. Women languished in the verbal relations department because their situation did not call for them to transfer their day to the group's consciousness. Maybe there lingers some jealousy there…

For years, women have been credited with higher verbal skills than men. Studies have suggested that female human beings possess higher verbal and linguistic skills than males. However, history tells us a different story. When asked to identify great speakers names like Patrick Henry, Abraham Lincoln, Winston Churchill, Franklin Roosevelt, Martin Luther King, John F. Kennedy, Malcolm X, Abbie Hoffman, and Ronald Reagan come to mind. Not just great speeches but great quotes seem to reside in the male half of the species. Consider some of the following:

"There is nothing impossible to him who will try." - *Alexander the Great*

"I came, I saw, I conquered." - *Julius Caesar*

"Turn the other cheek." - *Jesus Christ*

"There is nothing to fear, but fear itself."- *Franklin D. Roosevelt*

"Some men see things as they are and say, 'Why?' I dream of things that never were and say, 'Why not?'" - *George Bernard Shaw*

"Ask not what your country can do for you, but what you can do for your country." - *John Kennedy*

"Why do I fight? Because I can't sing or dance. Yo!" – *Rocky Balboa*

"This is one small step for a man, one giant leap for mankind." -*Neil Armstrong*

The list goes on. And for the women? Those beings that have been credited with the premier knowledge of human verbal interaction? It is tough to find a quote that comes from a famous woman. Well, there is usually only one universal quote attributed to womankind. That, of course, is Marie Antoinette's famous line, when told that her countrymen had no food, she so eloquently said,

"Let them eat cake."

So where are the verbal skills that women allegedly possess? Why are they as notoriously absent from everyday conversation as they are from the literary record? Are you drunk enough now to hear what may be the truth? If not take a long gulp (or throw this book in the trash!). Ponder the idea, for argument's sake, that women are able to express themselves verbally on a higher level than men. The undying need of the human spirit is to be heard. Right? Has there been a worldwide conspiracy for the last 10,000 years designed to keep women, "in their place". Plausible? I don't think so. How about another reason? Women feel better about themselves than men do. They accept their role in society. They are so happy with who they are that they do not feel the need to stand up at the campfire and brag about their exploits. They listen to you go on and on about the office, the hunt for Mastodon, or the conquest of the New World, and they don't say anything. They just listen. They don't compete, they don't try to outdo you. They listen. They cheer you on. Go get 'em, Sparky! They feel good when you feel good. They are sad when you are sad. They understand that they have an indispensable role in society and they don't argue this role. They are different than men and they are okay with that. What a crock! I was just screwing with you. Drink up and let's get back to reality.

So, is there a conspiracy to keep women down? I don't think so, at least not a conspiracy in the true sense. But it is the nature of men to *out-talk*, *out-perform* and generally *out-do* women. We like to impress women but somewhere along the line men went from impressing women to subjugating them. Maybe we thought that we had to keep impressing them or they would leave us. We are threatened by it. Most women can't outrun you, lift more weights than you do, or beat you in video games. And the ones that can? Well, you can't stand those dykes now, can you? Sorry, I went off again. Now, let's get back to our story.

Girls are tested at a young age on words that they pick up from their teacher. While young boys are fighting the urge to explore the playground, young girls are happy to sit and listen to what the female teacher has to say. When the "verbal" test is administered, the young girls are able to score higher because they simply have a better vocabulary than boys. They have an advantage over boys because girls read at a younger age than boys do. For years, it was thought that reading was a skill of identifying visual symbols. However, recent educational research has proven that reading is actually a process of hearing, not seeing. The structure of the female brain gives females an advantage in hearing. Hearing and learning new words take place in a special region on the left side of the brain. With the spoken word, the female clearly has the advantage. Boys are better at repeating and identifying the sounds of animals and cars. This may be the result of the adaptation to hunting while the male mind was evolving. Girls have the center of their brain adapted for words. Young girls seek the approval of their mentor so they try harder than young boys do. Boys are busy trying to find a way to release the pent-up energy that sitting in a seat all day long has brought them.

While men depended on their communication skills for their very survival, there was no impetus for the evolution of female communication skills. Women just did not need to converse that much to get their point across to their comrades. The line of reasoning is that women do not communicate well because they never needed to communicate well. The female brain thinks in multiple directions when asked a question. Some of these directions are even contradictory to each other. They think about each outcome to the point that they do none of them. In contrast, a man will focus his energies on one outcome; learning alternative methods from his mistakes along the way, but sticking to the one focused goal that he has set for himself. This type of thinking reflects in the basic differences between male and female communication. Women will say one thing, while thinking something totally different. This leaves the male perplexed. Maybe it was meant to. She said yes- but meant no. On the other hand, did she say no -but mean yes? No. What? Drink your beer.

Remember, she is not only speaking differently than you, she is interpreting what you say poles apart from what you mean. Here is an example of such an interaction. I have attached the thought pattern in italics.

Happy Husband: Dear, what do you think about a movie tonight? *(I would like to go to the movies.)*
Wonder wife: That sounds good. *(I really do not want to go to the movies tonight. What will I wear?.)*
Happy Husband: What do you feel like seeing? *(I really want to know what she wants to see.)*
Wonder wife: Oh, I don't care. Whatever you want. *(He had better pick a movie that I want to see.)*
Happy Husband: What about that new war picture, I heard it is pretty good. *(It should be an interesting movie.)*
Wonder wife: That sounds good. *(Oh God, I cannot sit through another war movie!)*

Sound familiar? Women can communicate their feelings to other women. When it comes to communicating their feelings to men, women and men do not connect. She does not want to hurt your feelings. Men become frustrated because they do not understand the vocal strategies of women. Here is another example. Jason C. is an architect living in western North Carolina.

"I do not understand my wife. I am beginning to learn how to deal with it-but it is still very difficult to deal with her behavior. Whenever my wife is upset, she just stops talking to me. That would be fine but she stomps around the house - pounding her feet on the floor, slamming the doors just loud enough to be irritating, and cleaning or vacuuming in the room that I am sitting. This behavior will continue until I ask her what is wrong. Of course, she never answers me unless I ask at least three times. The first answer I get from her is "nothing" as she stomps out of the room. She returns a few minutes later, increasing her banging and excessive cleaning. I do not mind the cleaning, but it is only a matter of time before she breaks something. She does other stuff that is so childish- like not answering the phone or the door if someone knocks. I finally have to ask her a couple of times what is bothering her before she begins to fumble for the words to find. After much ado about nothing she finally tells me what is wrong. I have tried for years to get her to get in touch with her feelings, but I haven't got anywhere. I just deal with it a lot better now than I did when we were first married."

When a man is upset with his spouse he approaches her and explains what exactly it is that is bothering him. This may not happen in each relationship, but it is usually a characteristic of men to be direct and up front about their feelings. When a woman is upset with her spouse, Jason C.'s scenario is common. When upset, female humans usually close themselves off verbally, stomp around the house, and resort to slamming cabinets, doors, etc. One man reports that his ex-wife moved furniture every time she was upset. After rearranging the house five times in the first few months of marriage this guy caught on. It is not that men are not perceptive. It just takes them a little longer to understand. Drink your beer before I get into body language.

In a recent study men and women were shown pictures of models that were trying to show different emotions using their facial expressions. There was a difference in the determination of the emotions in the facial expression. Although there were similarities in the interpretation of the facial expressions, there were many deviations. As a group, women were more sensitive to happy faces than men were. However, men were more sensitive to sad expressions in another man's face than were women. And by contrast, men were less sensitive to sad faces in other women. A women's face had to be very sad before a man noticed. The study suggests that women are not as sensitive to the facial expressions of men as men are to other men. Interesting?

Ω

Men have had a dual role in society for the last 10,000 years. The first is to advance society. To increase the ways that thoughts and ideas are transmitted to other men for the betterment of the species. The second is to gain favor with a woman. Most men say that they are one out of two. Has the point been made? Men and women have developed a complex communication over the millennia; it is just not with each other. But why? Are the sexes that different? Are there physiological differences that make men and women almost separate species? In our next chapter, we will examine the reasons for this difference. How many beers did you drink?

Finish your beer and stop hating your ex-wife.

2

Our Brains are Different

Appetizer
Jose Cuervo Tequila

Main Course
Yuengling

It is widely accepted today that the brain is the "command center" of the body. One of the main functions of the brain is to interpret signals from the outside world and respond appropriately to those signals. What we hear, see, taste, smell, and touch is all filtered through our brain. Experience tells us what to do with the information. Some experiences tell us what not to do. Our grasp on reality is directly related to our brain's interpretation of our surroundings. Could you imagine what would happen if our brain did not send the signal to remove your hand from a hot stove? Or if your ancestors did not run from that saber-toothed lion? Each one of us is the outcome of millions of years of natural selection; and for humans that means natural selection for intelligence. The smartest brains interpreted the world in a manner that would allow the owner to live, bear young, and raise the young to an age where the young could successfully reproduce. What constitutes the human brain? The brain is a grayish mass of neurons, synapses, and various biological compounds. Are the male and female brains the same? Despite what champions of the Women's Liberation Movement want you to think – no, they are different. Very different. This difference begins while humans are embryos in the uterus and continues well into senescence. It is the knowledge of these differences that will help The Drinking Man understand women.

Human beings have been researching the brain for thousands of years. Cave paintings show holes being bored in the skulls of cave dwellers from Neolithic times, around 9000 years ago. In addition to the mystical reasons of letting out bad spirits; scientists hypothesize that early man performed this procedure to cure everything from migraines to epilepsy. Hippocrates detailed the practice of brain surgery throughout Greek history. The Incas practiced brain surgery; skeletons of some Incan skeletons actually showed healing of the bone (which indicates the patient survived the procedure). Leonard Da Vinci's extensive collection of brain drawings chronicled awareness of the brain in his time. Vivisectionists and physicians of the Dark Ages cleared the way for today's knowledge of brain function. Stories such as Frankenstein showed the interest in the brain and its effect on behavior during the nineteenth century. Sigmund Freud, B. F. Skinner, and others provided the basic behavioral studies of the brain that college kids study today. The U.S. Army used unwitting soldiers in its experiments in the 1940's and 1950's on the effect of different hallucinogens on human behavior. Popular research in the 1960's and 1970's consisted of studying the behaviors of people that had suffered various types of brain damage. The damaged part of the brain was linked to the intellectual deficiencies in the injured person. Drink your beer.

There are a few standard methods that scientists rely on to show brain function and physiology. One classic method is tomography. Tomography is the slicing of the brain into thin sheets (sort of like roast beef at the deli counter). In the old days scientists had to discolor the sliver with a variety of messy stains to bring out the various morphological aspects of the brain. Scientists stared through a microscope at these discolored slides to observe the slightest brain variance. Now, with computer-enhanced imaging, the slices can be fed into a computer and colorized, polarized, digitized, leaving the scientist mesmerized with an enhanced image to study. These images can be defined according to the areas of the brain, types of cell, numbers and forms of neurons, information on nerve cell connections and various other attributes. The image can be analyzed for cell thickness, region thickness, and volume. This information is used to tell the difference in male and female brains. This method is somewhat invasive and can be deleterious to a living subject because the brain must be removed and sliced into sections to obtain results. It's hard to get over that. Techniques that are more modern include non-invasive functional imaging processes such as PET (Positron Emission Topography) MRI (Magnetic Resonance Imaging) and/or Brain Topographic Electroencephalography.

The latest techniques that scientists use to study the brain are a type of three-dimensional x-rays. The MRI can follow where the blood is flowing in the brain when a question is asked of, or a task assigned to, the subject. Therefore, the specific part of the brain a person uses to think is determined by following blood flow into that particular region of the brain. In both PET and MRI, analysts can see where the brain is processing information by following the biological systems of the brain. During these tests, a radioactive tracer is injected into the subject and the specific machine utilized catalogues the movement of the tracer. The camera records the pictures and turns them into an image for the researcher to examine. In some cases, the PET and the MRI are used in conjunction with each other to verify and enhance the results from either device. The beauty of the non-invasive techniques is that you can use them to image how men and women(live men and women!) think. The technology allows researchers to follow the thought processes as the subjects perform tasks, calculate mathematical problems, answer questions and solve problems of every sort. These techniques are used to document the differences in thinking between men and women when performing similar actions. (Any man has spent more than an hour with a woman, realizes that there is a difference in the way the two sexes think. But scientists have given the idea credibility.) Using PET, blood flow to the brain can be measured while a person is conscious and awake. When a subject is thinking, the blood flows to the part of the brain that is being utilized for the thought process. PET scans follow the amount of glucose uptake in the brain. Remember that the subject must be injected with a radioactive marker for the specific device to read the results. Simply put, the part of the brain that is absorbing glucose is the area of the brain that is being used. Total blood flow to the brain increases during cerebral exercise. For example, while a person is undergoing a PET scan he or she is asked a question that requires a verbal response. The blood flows to the left side of the brain. If the person is asked a task that requires them to picture something in three-dimensional space the blood flows to the right side of the brain. This is a generalization for the human species. In reality, males and females, when asked the same question, will use different parts of their brain to respond to the same inquiry. This manner of thinking begins early in the development of a human being. It begins while the person is still an embryo. Let us look at early fetal development and then support our theories with the results from the new technologies of MRI and PET computer assisted imaging.

Drink your beer. (Isn't science wonderful?)

Sex differences in the brain begin in the uterus. As soon as their testicles are developed, a male embryo begins producing testosterone. The testosterone molecule will attach itself to brain tissue, making the brain different than the developing female embryonic counterpart. The male embryo is totally "masculinized" around the fifth month of pregnancy. Israeli Scientists Reuwen and Achiron have found that if you do an ultrasound examination when a woman is five months pregnant, you can distinguish a female brain from a male brain. A huge testosterone surge that begins around the seventh week changes the neural network. The neurons are laid down differently in males than females. The brain cells form separate patterns in different parts of the brain in males than they do in females. Men have more neurons, the brain is bigger, and there are more connections between the neurons. The effect of testosterone change is permanently welded on a males' brain. Research shows that the male brain will not revert to its former female state after this initiation has taken place. The change is irreversible. If male rats are castrated in later life, they still cogitate like other intact males. This may be why the eunuchs of Rome enjoyed their job. After masculinization, the male brain is the male brain even in the absence of testosterone. In one experiment, scientists tried try to reverse the masculinization of the newborn brain. Professors Mack, Given, et al, delivered laboratory rats by Caesarean section and castrated the males immediately (talk about a slap to get you breathing!). Even though he was no longer producing testosterone, the castrated rat's brain remained masculinized throughout life. Therefore, the differences in male/female thinking remain throughout life. The effect of testosterone has changed the Drinking Man forever. Now he must understand what these differences are so that he may understand his female companions. Drink your beer.

Ω

Long before they are born, men think like men. Women think like women. In a study led by Richard Haier, Professor of Psychology at the University of New Mexico, Magnetic Resonance Imaging (MRI) pictures of the brain were used to determine morphological differences between the male and female brain. Haier deems that the differences noted in his study show that the human brain has evolved into two separate brains. The male brain and the female brain. Creationists usually take the same stance. When God created Eve why did he change the mold? Was it to improve upon an earlier design? Or to make it different? Evolutionists and Creationists agree on very little. One thing they do agree upon is the difference between male and female thinking.

Haier's study shows that men have 6.5 times more gray matter than women do. Gray matter receives input from the outside world and processes this information. Consider this mathematical comparison. If you were 6.5 times taller than a friend of yours that was six feet tall, you would be thirty-nine feet tall. A person that weighed one hundred and fifty pounds would weigh nine hundred and seventy five pounds. That is significant and accounts for the difference in intelligence levels between men and women. Men are 6.5 times more "different" than women. That is not the end of the study. Haier also found that the gray matter is distributed differently in men and women. In women, a majority of the gray matter (at least 84%) was found in the brain's frontal lobes, whereas in males only 45 % of gray matter is located in the frontal lobes. The remainder of the gray matter in males is distributed throughout the brain. In addition, the gray matter is located in different parts of the male brain. Women solve problems with their frontal lobes only; men use their whole brain and are able to call on a larger area of their brain to "connect the dots" and solve problems in a more intelligent, logical manner. It is as if a man can go to many different retail outlets to buy the supplies he needs, women can only shop at one store. According to neural imaging, men have a higher overall amount of glucose uptake than women. However, the interesting part is the variations in thinking that men and women experience. Men have higher activity in the parts of the brain that are involved in physical activity. That women have lower activity in this part of the brain is not surprising. Women are less active than men are. In one experiment men and women were asked to do simple tasks dealing with word meaning and usage. As the subjects responded to these tasks, the blood flow to their brain was monitored. During a verbal task men use the left frontal lobe of their brain to answer the question. For the same question, women use both the right and left frontal lobes. This difference in processing words shows that men and women use language differently on a biological level.

We can go to a local schoolyard and see that boys and girls behave differently, starting at a young age. Is this behavior the result of societal conditioning? Opponents to the idea that the male and female brain are different say that society conditioned young boys and girls to behave the way in a certain manner. If left alone, young boys and girls would behave in gender-neutral ways. It is the age-old "nature versus nurture" controversy. The idea was that society conditioned (nurtured) these young people to play with certain toys, responding negatively if the wrong sex picked up the wrong toy. Boys should not play with dolls. Nice girls do not shoot sparrows with BB guns from their bedroom window. There was quite a movement in the late sixties and early seventies amongst liberal females and feminized males to provide their children with gender-neutral toys and experiences. Guess what happened? When given the same toys boys made weapons and vehicles out of theirs, turning even the most mundane toy into a car or a pistol. The girls played house and acted as if their "toys" were interacting like humans. The "Everybody's the Same" movement did not lose hope; they just remained unsuccessfully focused on canceling the differences between boys and girls. They continue to this day trying to perpetuate the myth that young boys and girls are the same. You can find them at just about every family reunion. Their kids are the ones that do not know how to interact properly with your kids. Anyone that has children knows that, when given a choice, young boys will choose to play with trucks and cars. They will race them, crash them, and throw the vehicles off high "cliffs." Young females will have fun with dolls; playing house and dressing up the dolls. Animals "play" to practice their future survival roles. Young wolves wrestle and fight to prepare them for their future status in the pack. Lion cubs chase bugs and butterflies to hone their hunting skills. Fledgling birds flap their wings in preparation for flight. Human beings are mammals. Mammals are animals. Far be it for this writer to say that we are not part of the animal world. In addition, as animals, if we see our past, present, and future in biological terms we can become more secure in who we were, who we are, and who we are going to be.

Human children prepare for the roles they will play in life by playing with toys. Little boys play with airplanes, fire trucks, and boats in preparation for their future as pilots, firefighters, and captains of aircraft carriers. Little boys make tin can "walkie-talkies" to prepare for their roles as radio announcers, singers, and inventors of communication devices. Little boys play with pretend weapons to prepare themselves to defend their home, their honor, and their country. Little boys play baseball, football, hockey, basketball and other sports to test their physical bodies and prepare themselves for a future as team players. Little boys make forts and tree houses to prepare themselves to be builders and architects. Little boys practice with musical instruments for hours to prepare themselves to be prodigies, virtuosos, and rock stars.

Little girls play house.

Drink your beer

Ω

There are differences in nature for a reason. From a huge diversity of traits and behaviors, nature selects for those that are the most advantageous for the species. There are differences between men and women in how they view time, determine the speed of an object, perform math calculations, and visual spatializations (how well the mind orients objects in three dimensions) for a reason. Moreover, the reason is simple. Due to the action of testosterone the male mind is different than the female mind in all aspects. This may explain why men become mathematicians, pilots, engineers, architects, Presidents, Generals, songwriters, race car drivers, astronauts, chefs, painters, sculptors, and just about every other profession that requires a different thought.

In a computerized maze-searching experiment by Scott Mowatt of Wayne State University in Detroit, Mowatt found that it took females five minutes longer to find their way out of the maze than their male counterparts. This, of course does not sit well with the "We Are All the Same" feminists. We are not all the same. Male rats are more adept at finding their way in the maze; female rats are better at taking care of children.

Ω

One of the "advances" of the Equal Rights movements was to allow women to serve in more positions in the military. The list of male war heroes is endless. The female brain did not develop to protect their tribe. The female mind did not evolve to invent weapons to defend a nation, never mind lead men into battle using these weapons. The male mind evolved to do these tasks, while the female mind evolved to support the male and perpetuate the species. These differences in brain function do not mean men are better than women. It means men are different than women. Drink your beer.

Professors Tracy J. Schors of Rutgers University demonstrated that violent stress improves the learning curve of males, while it impairs comprehension in females. Stimulus such as delivering electrical shocks to a rat were used to test learning abilities under stress in both male and female rats. Schors experiment showed that when her team exposed male rats to electric shocks, connections between neurons in their hippocampus increased; and the rats learned new activities more rapidly. The female rats showed the opposite effect. When female rats were subjected to electric shocks, connections between neurons in their hippocampus decreased. The result was a decrease in the females' ability to navigate mazes or learn new tasks. This study demonstrates the way in which different genders respond under stress, and it has interesting implications for the ways male and female children should be taught in school. Exposure to the electric shock had opposite effects on learning, with the male rats showing an increase in cognitive abilities. Female rats exposed to these stresses showed a dramatic decrease in cognitive ability. In subsequent experiments, these same scientists confirmed that the beneficial effect of stress on learning in males depends on masculinization of the male brain, which occurs before birth. The scientists investigated further and demonstrated that by injecting the pregnant mother with an anti-testosterone drug (cyprotestosterone acetate, not found in the Drinking Man's medicine cabinet!) the male brain would not develop properly. Male rat pups born to mothers injected with the anti-testosterone drug showed no improvement in their learning in response to stress. The male characteristic of learning under stress was lost as a result of their exposure to the anti-testosterone drug while they were fetuses. The next group was male rats whose mothers did not receive any injections of the anti-testosterone drug. They exhibited the male characteristic of learning while under stress, despite having no testicles to produce testosterone. Those babies retained that male-typical characteristic, despite the fact that they could not make testosterone after birth.

Subscribing to the evolutionary theory of hunter-gathers it is not surprising to find that women do not visualize mentally in three dimensions, judge the speed of objects, or carry out mathematical calculations as well as men do. Most studies show that men and women are different in these categories. Does this account for the male dominated world? Contemplate this while you take a sip. A big sip.

As a fetus, and as a youth, the male brain develops at a slower pace. It takes more time to build something that is complex. Drawing a picture of a city is not as time consuming as building a three dimensional model in one-tenth scale. The female mind is the drawing; it is the template for the male brain. This is what accounts for the duality of the male brain. The female brain is at its physiologic roots. The male brain started out as female and became masculine from the effects of testosterone. Along with a myriad of other factors, this may account for the research that shows young boys lagging behind young girls in elementary school. During this time, the mind of the male is refining its neural network. In adolescence, young men surpass young women in most academic areas. Some research shows girls still have an edge on boys in the verbal/linguistic arena.

In females, the verbal skills are more diffused throughout the brain. Communication diffused throughout the brain allows for a processing of verbal content. When the processing is complete the response has been infused with emotion. Could this explain why women get upset easily? Biologically it seems to make sense. Socially, it makes even more sense.

In her book, "The Female Brain," Dr. Louann Brizendine explains how the female brain works, what women are thinking, and the different ways they process thoughts compared with the way men perform these same functions. Brizendine's research shows that a woman typically uses 20,000 words each day compared to a man's 7,000. What are women saying that it requires 13,000 more words each day? Some sort of secret algorithms that are explaining the meaning of life on an algebraic level? Are these words of science that no one but women can understand? Or could it be that women talk more and say less? If you understand, and accept, that difference you will have a happy marriage. Talking makes women feel good. Talking sends impulses through their emotional center and quiets their emotions. Biological research may have the answer to the "Riddle of the Thirteen Thousand".

Brizendine acknowledges that male and female brains are different in architecture and chemical composition. "Women have an eight-lane superhighway for processing emotion, while men have a small country road," she writes. Men, however, "have an O'Hare Airport as a hub for processing thoughts about sex, where women have the airfield nearby that lands small and private planes." A man's brain is larger with wiring that is more specialized for functions related to the world. In contrast, a women's brain, according to Brizendine, uses a tremendous amount of space for processing emotion and memory formation-and each time the female verbalizes anything, the words are processed through an extensive network of previous emotions and memories. Is this why women bring up arguments from months, even years, previous to the conversation they are in? Drink your beer and not a word of this to your spouse.

Ω

Herbert Lansdell is considered a pioneer in detailing the intellectual differences between men and women. Through the earlier work of other scientists, Lansdell knew that damage to the left temporal lobe would result in a loss of verbal skills in humans. In addition to speech itself, other verbal skills like recognizing the spoken or written word would also be affected. Lansdell found that women were less affected by damage to the left temporal lobe than men were. These studies showed that brain damaged, and normal people, tend to use one hemisphere of the brain more than the other for certain verbal tasks. Except in women. Independent scientists working in the area of brain function during that time confirmed these studies. One independent discovery was that of Jeannette McGlone, a graduate student at Dalhousie University in Halifax, Nova Scotia. McGlone also found that damage to the left hemisphere caused less observable damage in women than in men. McGlone's conclusion was that certain verbal skills are compartmentalized, more dependent on a certain area of the brain, in the male brain. In men, communication is direct and to the point. In the male brain, the communication section is located in a specific area. Verbal skills in men have been evolutionarily refined for millennia. Conversely, women's verbal skills are more diffusely spread throughout the female brain. More brain area is utilized in females for verbal interactions. It takes a longer time for women to process words. The words have been drenched by emotion instead of logic. When a man hears a directive, it goes straight to an area in his brain that is specialized to understand that directive. The man responds accordingly. According to the directive. When a woman hears a directive, the words are diffused throughout her brain. The journey through her brain takes longer than the male and has emotions attached to it that have nothing to do with the directive. The aforementioned directive is absorbed by the emotional centers on the journey to conscious thought. Like an driverless automobile careening off other vehicles, denting them, getting dented itself, so by the time the car is finished on its journey it is damaged, maybe unrecognizable. The woman hears the same words yet reacts much differently than the man. Her brain is not wired for logical action in *response* to speech. It is wired for emotion, *based* on speech. Learn this, Grasshopper, and your life will be much easier. This could explain the bewilderment that men feel when women totally sidestep the *content* of what they are saying and concentrate on the *tone* that the man is using. The oblivious male is confounded with the emphasis on his tone. To him this is trivial. To her it is not.

Different.

He is concerned with the direct meaning of his words. His words have come from a direct and localized part of his brain. The female hears him but his meaning is diffused through emotional filters that filter the content of what he is saying and focus on the emotion. The female focuses on the tone of his voice as the predisposing factor to her response. Women do not understand the thinking patterns of men. Men do not understand why women spend so much time on the emotional aspects of their speech. The communication gap between men and women appears to have a firm physiological basis. Is this transmission of thought linked to behavior? Do men trust men more than women? Let us explore that question. But first, take a sip.

A friend of mine was scheduled for a hernia operation. His family doctor recommended that he meet with the surgeon to have the procedure explained and answer any questions that he might have. My friends eyes opened wide when he heard that the doctor's first name was "Leslie" (last name withheld to protect privacy). My friend left his doctor's office and called me on his cell phone. He was frantic. The conversation went something like this:

"I am supposed to have my hernia operation next Thursday, and I ain't going!" he blurted raucously.

"Well, why not? I thought everything was set. Isn't it a minor procedure? Are you getting last minute jitters?" I probed inquisitively.

"It's not that. I just found out that the surgeon is a woman!" he whispered, barely audible.

"Oh, oh, yeah, um….well, uh, she must be…uh…like board certified, or something, right?" I stammered.

"Would you have a women perform surgery on you? Especially down there?" he pleaded.

"I, uh, gee, that's a tough one. No, probably not. Especially around the privates. You know how I feel about women and penis envy. 'Oops, sorry, I slipped!' is not a good enough excuse for me." I retorted.

"I am not doing it. I'll grow three nuts before I let some girl doctor with 'Daddy issues' around my johnson while I am knocked out." he yapped.

"Daddy issues?"

"Yes, she's a woman in a man's job. Therefore, she has Daddy issues. Period."

"Are you saying that female doctors choose medicine because they have Daddy issues?"

"Yes, why else would they not choose to be a nurse like regular women?" he answered questioningly with affirmation.

"Well, good luck with it." I said, "Let me know what three nuts feel like!"

When my comrade called his doctor back, he was pleasantly embarrassed to find out that Leslie was a male doctor. The surgery went fine and we were disappointed that we did not get to call him E.T. (the Extra-Testicle!) The question of female surgical competence was out the back door, returning to the atmosphere of happy hours and dinner parties, floating unseen throughout hospitals and casual conversations alike. Nevertheless, the question remains. Are women doctors as trustworthy as male doctors are? Does the female mind lend itself to the fast decisions and spatial visualization required of a surgeon? I am only asking the questions. With the small percent of females that opt to become surgeons a good longitudinal study has yet to be performed. One of the last things most people want is someone having a "hot flash" while doing surgery on even the least obtrusive part of their body. Take a big sip this is about to get very honest.

Ω

From early caveman days and right up until the present day, men have physically dominated women. Not much discussion in that area. The widespread notion was that insecure men had to keep women suppressed. Bras were seen as the ultimate male control device. He had to hide those breasts so that other men could not see them. After centuries of repression, women fought back. They sought equality. They wanted rights. They were not going to take it anymore. Bras were burned- the boobie was free. During all of the social upheaval of the sixties, the Woman's Liberation Movement leaped forward and gained steam. Women lobbied to enter into historically male professions. They wanted to be doctors, lawyers, and police officers. Therefore, the rigid society that had kept women back for millennia relaxed its standards. Women could now enter into these fields. Not only could they enter but also they were given advantages. Quotas were kept that allowed women to occupy seats that would have gone to males that are more qualified. Affirmative action started in the late sixties. We were all going to be equal. Men were no longer the dominant species. Well, here we are fifty years later and what do we have? Do women doctors dominate the medical field? Is the military run by Amazons with AK-47's? Are politicians, that bastion of expression and communication, solely a haven for women? Not really. What has happened is that women have flooded into fields where they can excel. There has been a huge rise in strip joints, whorehouses, and massage parlors. Have you looked at the internet lately? Is it saturated with site after site of female neurosurgeons? Not quite. The internet is flooded with naked women of every kind. Women have been liberated to be themselves. More about that in a later chapter.

But that does not mean that women are inferior to men in all cognitive areas? Of course not. According to Harvard University sociobiologist, Edward O. Wilson, women are better than men in many categories. But women are women and men are men. Viva la difference. Drink your beer.

Ω

Don't forget that without women we wouldn't be here. Nor would we want to.

3

The Female Sexual Strategy

Appetizer
Captain Morgan Spiced Rum

Main Course
Yuengling

The true function of any female organism from fruit-fly to human being is to perpetuate the species. Animal species use various reproductive strategies to achieve this goal. In nature, the breeding strategy of a creature helps to ensure the survival of the offspring. Sheep mate in the fall so they can give birth in the spring. This allows the lambs to be born into a warm environment with plenty of food. Sea turtles lay hundreds of eggs, then leave the eggs to fend for themselves. One out of a thousand sea turtle hatchlings will make it to adulthood. Do human beings have a reproductive strategy? Are there certain biological rituals that humans practice? Or has civilization eclipsed the need for a biological reproductive strategy in human beings? Shall we compare the male and female reproductive strategies of various organisms, including human beings?

The human male can produce several hundred million sperm each day. Roughly fifty million sperm are released each time the male ejaculates. These sperm are manufactured in a one hundred twenty-five yard long network of tubes called the seminiferous tubules; which are found in the testes. Over a lifetime, that adds up to billions of happy sperm. Out of fifty million competitors, one sperm makes the seven inch journey through the vagina and uterus to fertilize the egg in the least amount of time. It has won the sperm race. Moreover, that sperm was you. Awww… Right from the start, you were a winner. Go ahead, take a drink for that one.

No matter how fat and slow we have become, all human beings can feel good that, at one time, they were number one in a race of over fifty million! Not only that, they made the right choice by traveling up the right fallopian tube (while twenty five million other sperm went the wrong way!).

This is a quite a feat when you consider that the average sperm is microscopic. As soon as it is ejected, the sperm takes control of it's situation. There are millions of them and only the strongest make it to the egg. The weak defective sperm will swim hopelessly against the vaginal walls while the strong sperm swim the seven inches to the egg. And sperm are troopers. They do not know if there is an egg, or even if the female is ovulating. However, they go anyway, kind of like the Marines. No guarantee, just the promise of a tough journey ahead of them. Oorah! And what a journey it is! The average sperm is only thousandths of an inch long(.0023 of an inch to be exact.) That means it would take four hundred thirty five of them to total one inch. As stated previously, the journey is approximately seven inches to the egg. That calculates out to approximately three thousand forty-five sperm lengths. Using the same ratio with a six-foot human male, he would have to swim 18,270 feet (3.46 miles) underwater, holding their breath! That would encompass a free dive to the wreck of the Titanic, which lies in water 2.5 miles down, and then another mile swim to the side.

The human female produces one egg each month, and it is going nowhere. It just sits there, waiting for the sperm. (Analogous?) If the sperm fails to show, the egg will let go and slough off into a five-day session of bleeding and hormonal release. However, the egg is a scarce commodity. Over her reproductive life the average female, starting at age 12, and ending at age forty-two, will produce (30 years times 12 months/eggs each year) 360 eggs. That is the biology; the reality is that human females usually become pregnant between the ages of twenty to thirty years old. Ten years. That is only 120 eggs. Moreover, not every egg will be fertilized. Of the eggs that are fertilized, only one out of three will grow to produce a viable fetus. Therefore, we have a basic difference in what makes a successful reproductive strategy for human males and human females. Males gametes far outnumber female gametes. There are fifty million sperm in each ejaculate. But what if a man ejaculates twice? Or three times. Some young bucks can do this daily, older bucks monthly. In just one male the number of sperm produced monthly, and ejaculated, is in the billions. Compared to one lonely egg sitting attached to the uterine wall. There is a discrepancy here. Drink up, it gets complicated.

A successful breeding strategy requires the organism to mate and it's offspring live long enough to reproduce. So what makes a human male a successful breeder? Inseminating as many women as possible? Is it a numbers game? Has Mother Nature selected for this behavior? How does a male know which females are ready for mating? Many would say that the first clue that a female is receptive is visual. Hence, the male preoccupation with "checking out" as many females as possible. It is hardwired into the primitive portion of the male brain to seek out women that are displaying "I am ready" behaviors. These include excessive movement, smiling, staring back at the male, lack of clothing, and touching their skin. Does wearing a thong satisfy the basic primate drive to expose her buttocks? Figure that out on your own. Once the male sees these behaviors he becomes physically, and psychologically, aroused. A male will next attempt to inseminate each of these females. In the caveman days, it was a simple act of approaching the female and jostling around (or hitting her over the head with a club). The act required minimal foreplay. (Foreplay? Naaa, I refuse to open that can of worms!) The first pickup lines probably went something like this.

> Caveman: "Uhnn?"
> Cavewoman: "Uhn?"
> Caveman: "Uhnnn?"
> Cavewoman: " Uhuh..unn…"
> Caveman: "Uhn! Uh! Uhn!"
> Cavewoman: " Uhuh! Uhuh! Uhuh! Uhn! Uhn!"
> Caveman: "Uhn! Eeee. Uh! Uhn!"
> Cavewoman: " Uhuh! Uhuh! Uhuh!"
> Caveman: "Uhn! Oh. Eeeh. Oooh. Oooh. !"
> Cavewoman: " Uhuh! Uhuh! Uhuh! Uhuh!
>   Uhuh!"
> Caveman: "Oooh. Oooh. Eeeh. Eeeh. Uhn!
>   Uhn! Uhnnnnn…..."(at this point the
>   male would either go to sleep, or
>   leave the "scene of the crime".)
> Cavewoman: "Huh?"

Then the act was over. The temporary distraction of mating caused the male to drop his vigilance concerning the dangers of the wild. No time for cuddling. (Sound familiar?) Once he was "done" he had to reassess the location. He had to get up and see what was in his immediate area that could cause him harm. He would look around for anything that was attracted by the activity. Saber-toothed tigers? Other human males? Large predatory birds? Plus- he was hungry. This is the root of human males reproductive behavior. If he could do this a few times a week, he would be reproductively successful. Promiscuity is a successful male strategy for increasing his genetic propagation in the world. This is evidenced by anyone that has ever lived on a farm.

A bull will mate with a cow for a few days – and then lose interest in mating. That is, until another cow comes along. Then he will begin his amorous activities anew. This holds true for most farm critters. The mating wanes until a new partner is introduced. David Jessel in *"Brain Sex: The Real Difference Between Men and Women,"* refers to the mating behaviors that is witnessed in farm animals as the "Coolidge Effect". The name is attributed to remarks made when Calvin Coolidge and his wife visited a government farm when he was President. As the Presidential party passed the chicken coops, Mrs. Coolidge witnessed a rooster repeatedly mounting a hen. She asked her aide how often the rooster copulated each day.

"Dozens of times," was the reply from her aide.

"Tell that to the President," Mrs. Coolidge requested.

When the President passed by, seconds later, and was told about the rooster and Mrs. Coolidge's response, Coolidge asked,

"Is it with the same hen every time?"

"Oh no, Mr. President, it is with a different hen each time." came the answer. The President nodded slowly, then said,

"Tell that to Mrs. Coolidge...."

Jessel believes that the male of the species has an innate desire for sexual novelty. This desire is testosterone-based and present throughout a man's life. Don't even think about it, you're not a cave man- or a farm animal. Just drink your beer and keep reading.

Alfred Kinsey, in his famous study on human sexuality, Sexual Behavior in the Human Male (1948) and Sexual Behavior in the Human Female (1953) reported that men enthusiastically pursue sexual diversity. The amorous activities of men that have elevated themselves to a position of power lays credence to this theory. Famous men throughout history have been known for their aptitude to inseminate multiple women. Sultans kept harems. Harems with dozens of waiting females. These females had to be guarded to keep them from following their natural path to reproduction. Eunuchs (castrated males) kept the women captive. Men without testicles that kept the sultan's woman chaste or they were exterminated. One historical figure that comes to mind when you think of the promiscuity of powerful men is Genghis Khan.

Genghis Khan was a powerful emperor and ruthless conqueror in the 13th century. A study done by an international group of geneticists has estimated that approximately sixteen million men alive today can trace their Y chromosome back to the great Khan himself. The study was performed by taking blood samples from men in the former ruler's Mongolian empire. It was found that 8 % of the men tested carried the Y chromosome of Genghis Khan. This number adds up to 0.5% of the men in the entire world. It is the male that leaves his DNA in as many females as possible that is considered a reproductive success. However, what of the average guy during Khan's day? Did he get laid also? Probably, but not with as many different females. The same was true back in caveman days. Some men got laid a lot more than others. This is the starting point of the human male's sexual behavior. Take a drink and read on. She will still be there in fifteen minutes.

Ω

For argument's sake, let's agree that cavemen were horny. The sight of an amorous female would send them into a frenzy of enhanced sexuality. Depending on the strength and status of each male, they would take turns inseminating the "lucky" female cave woman. When the female became pregnant, and gave birth, each male would smile and grunt as follows:

"Ugh!" (Translation) – "he's got my eyes" or

"Ehf. Fah, guf! (Translation) - "look at the wang on that one, he's definitely my boy!" or

"Oofp. Bix!" (Translation) – "oh, jeez, another mouth to feed, let's go hunting."

The beginnings of the complexity of human sexuality were emerging. Some males would be stronger, faster, more attractive, better hung, able to "get it up" quicker after depositing his future in the female. Other males were too slow; too ugly, too poorly hung, and too limp to successfully compete for females. These pecker-challenged cavemen learned to release sexual tension through watching or ejaculating quickly before the female, in her orgasm-induced sleep, would awake. The rest of the male population fell somewhere along this continuum(That is us, guys!) and did what we could to reproduce.

Now the female cave dweller also had a strategy. She had one little precious egg each month. That egg was fertile for less than one week. The rest of that month she was either bleeding (one week), bloated (another week), or feeling sorry for herself (just a week?). In order to be reproductively successful, and satisfy her strong desire to bear children, a female had to attract a male, entice him to mate with her, and become pregnant. Then her life became a little more involved. During the pregnancy, the female was somewhat incapacitated. She had to be given extra food, care and protection during the pregnancy. This had to be provided by the male. Theoretically, by the father of her child. And where was he? Out impregnating other women! Therefore, women learned early on that one man could not be counted on to help her reproduce successfully. She also learned early on that men liked to think that they were the only ones having sex with her. Consequently, the reproductively successful female needed to convince more than one male that the child was his. So cavewoman became "Cave Harlot" sexually engulfing one man. Trying to draw all of his sexual energy from him so that he would not seek to have sex with other females. Remember how adventurous your ex-wife was before she got pregnant? That was no accident, fellas. It is a strategy that has served women for ten thousand years. Well, sooner or later, our little cave concubine would become pregnant. Feeling her mates "turn off" at her swollen midsection, Cave Harlot took her man orally. Caveman fell asleep. You figure out the rest. Drink quickly and rinse before we move on.

After a while, though, the caveman would stray. It was a biological need for him to seek out other women. Cave Harlot would be left alone, unable to hunt, or care for her newborn. Unless? Hey...Who was that caveman over there? Small member, never seems to get laid? She smiled, he smiled, and love was in the air. Now while her man was out sowing his seed amongst the clan, or hunting, the caveman with the small equipment would bring her food. He was not attractive to other females, could not hunt big game worth a dang, but he sure could bring home a little extra rabbit meat or other small animal when needed. And if one could help protect her and feed her – what about two? What about a random series of encounters so that many males would think they were the father of her child? In this scenario, the strongest "alpha" male would overtly keep other males away. Then again, when he was not looking, Cave Harlot would smile in her lover's direction affirming the connection that this may be your baby. For that reason, it became a part of the reproductive strategy of women to sleep around. This behavior exists even in modern times. How many marriages have been dissolved because of female infidelity? It is her need to feel attractive to many males that is the foundation for her cheating ways. Did you really think you were the first one to go through this? Drink up.

Consider divorce laws in the United States (and the rest of the "civilized" world). The laws give the female everything- the house, the kids, and half the money. We have socially evolved to accommodate Cave Harlot's strategy. She can now legally follow her biological nature to have many men supporting her children. It is too enticing for women in modern society to *not* get divorced. She can throw out her fat, balding, boring husband, while he still pays for the house and kids, and she gets to enjoy the attention of other males. Is it any wonder that the divorce rate is so high? We push women into divorce in America with the reckless appeal to her basal instinctive demons. Divorce laws guarantee that females will be happier, richer, and lead a more exciting life than they did while married. Is this a subconscious acceptance of the true nature of the human female? Many societies do not allow women to apply for divorce. We call these societies "third world" and "backward". Yet they are sophisticated enough to understand that women should not be allowed to follow their basic instincts. In our advanced, liberated society, we hide behind a false sense of superiority while we allow the basic structure of our social order to be whittled away by the primeval sexual strategy of women. Drink, chug, and open another one. It's going to get ugly.

Ω

British zoologists, Mark Beillis and Robin Baker of the University of Manchester, believe the female sexual strategy is part of the evolution of human beings. They have studied the deceptive female strategy. They propose that females mate with several males within a small span of days to better their reproductive success. This behavior allows the female to match up the sperm of different males against each other in her reproductive tracts. A "Battle of the Fallopian Tubes" between different sperm from different men. In this strategy, the female guarantees that the best quality sperm fertilizes her valuable egg. Not just the fastest sperm from one man. The fastest sperm of a fat dumbass is, uh, the fastest sperm of a fat dumbass. Women do not have to copulate as often as men to be reproductively successful. She can remain aloof and increase the sexual tension between herself and several males. As sexual tension increases males tend to produce more semen. More semen carries more sperm a greater distance. The number of times she copulates in a short time period is not as important as the quantity of the ejaculate. However, if quality, rather than quantity, of partners is important to a female, why does she not seek the best male she can, and stick with him? Beillis and Baker suggest that a female is unfaithful in order to persuade a second male to help rear her offspring. In short, if a female bears children by a range of possible fathers, she increases their genetic variability, maximizing the chance that at least some will succeed. The dinosaurs died out because they were unable to adapt to a changing world. Genetic variability is the evolutionary way to keep life moving forward. Beillis and Baker offer a cellular solution to the strategy of Cave Harlot and her multiple males. Very few human beings can make a claim of being strictly monogamous. Not too many people can argue against that statement. In addition to looks, and physical ability, females may mate with multiple partners as a way to pass on the genes for good quality sperm. Yes, we have returned to those little swimming haploid zygote makers. Let's see why.

Human sperm can live three to five days in the female reproductive tract. This is why men that catch their wives cheating are sickened when the female reveals that she was sleeping with her lover within days, or even hours, of her husband. Mating with her second male within the three to five days that her husband had sex with her increases the number of sperm that are vying for the egg. In contradiction to previous scientific dogma, the egg is not fertilized instantaneously in human females. The more semen deposited in the vagina, the greater the amount of fluid for the sperm to swim in. It takes a few days for the sperm to find their way into the cervix, pick a Fallopian tube, and out-swim the competing sperm. Beillis and Baker suggest that the female acts in a way that encourages competition between the sperm of different males. She strives to keep the sperm in her reproductive tract during this time. Beillis and Baker conclude that in face of natural selection, infidelity is as advantageous to female as it is to males, and that females time their sexual behavior in order to maximize the competitive abilities inherited by their offspring. It may take two to tango- but in evolutionary terms, it is the female that names the tune. Ready? Let's talk about the sperm. But take another drink first, it'll come in handy.

Ω

Sperm. The tiny homunculus. That one celled marvel of evolution. Let us not discount the survival instincts of sperm. Can we anthropomorphize this tiny, one-celled being? For discussion sake, let us say that sperm have a conscience. They have a purpose. Maureen Dowd, in her book, "Are Men Necessary?" alludes to the idea that men are an evolutionary dead end. The existence of sperm disproves that hypothesis. A tiny living creature that is able to swim, seek a goal, coordinate with other sperm, and avoid harsh conditions. The female egg just sits there, waiting for the sperm to make it complete. The complicated life of a sperm is just starting to be understood. Scientists do not agree on how long a sperm can live. Sperm are an evolutionary step-up, compared to the lifeless blob of protoplasm and DNA that an egg is. That sperm has evolved and is akin to higher forms of life – kind of like comparing an amoeba to a tuna fish. The tuna is much more evolved, able to school, use the school to survive and protect itself while looking out for each other. Sperm do the same. They work as a team. They compete with each other. The most able sperm will automatically try to fertilize any female. If this trait is inheritable, she will have more successful sons than other females and the behavior will spread throughout the species.

To test this theory, Beillis and Baker compiled a questionnaire to quiz woman on their infidelity. The researchers received replies from more than three thousand sexually active women. Out of these, eleven hundred and sixty two had copulated with someone other than their regular partner in the last five days. Beillis believes that the female mates outside the normal pair bond for a reason. One reason is to gain extra help in raising the young. Either in protection, or nurturing. For this reason, it is important that the "second male" believes that he has a genetic stake in the offspring. Whether or not he actually fertilizes her is not important to the female. She may even copulate with other males besides number one and number two. Three and four. Five, six, seven, eight? They may all look like good fathers. Strong, able, good providers. It helps her reproductive success to mate with all of them. She may have even mated with these suitors during infertile stages of her menstrual cycle. Just to throw them off. Heck, they have no perception when she is ovulating. Nor do they care. Until she starts to show that she is pregnant. It would make sense that the female would mate continuously to throw each male off, making them all think that they were the real father. When they studied the results of their questionnaire, Beillis and Baker, found that this was not the case. The women did not mate randomly during their menstrual cycle. They found that most women were unfaithful during their most fertile period, just before ovulation. This leads up to a different theory. One of "The Warrior Sperm".

Bellis and Baker looked at the infidelities that occurred within five days of the last mating with the husband. The predominance of evidence showed that females copulated with different males frequently within five days of each other. Human sperm can live for three to five days in the female reproductive tract. If the female egg is to be fertilized by the fittest sperm, she must have many of the little swimmers in her reproductive tract at the same time. It is only then that they can compete against each other.

What the researchers found was that the promiscuous females would mate with her lover within five days of mating with her regular partner. Her husband 'porked' her on Sunday, and Harry at the office nailed her in the copy room on Tuesday. She came home later than usual that night and went straight to the shower. Yuck. Now she has two opposing Sperm Armies inside her. You cannot have a war with only one army. Some women may go as far as to have three or more Sperm Armies in her at once. Beyond the "Gang Bang" sites on the internet, this may be a successful reproductive strategy for the human female. There are two factors at play here. The female is choosing a physical specimen that she thinks would make good brood stock. His physical features are what appeals to her. She entices him over. He chases her until she catches him. She invites him to inject his millions of sperm warriors into her reproductive battleground. The hypothesis was that the female acts in a way that encourages competition between the sperm of different males. Darwinian survival of the fittest. This promiscuous behavior depends on the female receiving sperm by the second male. These sperm will actually battle the sperm of the primary male. It is not only the quality and quantity of sperm that enables a man to father a child. It is the ability of his sperm to fight foreign sperm on the battleground of the female reproductive tract. Take a long drink of your beer; yuck..it's warm, throw it out and open another.

Sperm that fight against each other is a relatively new concept. Sperm analysis has been mostly subjective for the last twenty years. Imagine scientists observing sperm under a microscope for hours on end. They watched the tadpole-like maneuvers and concluded that most sperm were furiously whipping their tails in a blind attempt to be the first to reach the egg. One huge Boston Marathon with hundreds of millions of competitors. This is the most common notion of sperm behavior. Taught in college biology classes to the giggles and wisecracks of generations of students. However, with the aid of computers we can now plot the movement of sperm without the subjective bias of the scientist. Computer-aided sperm analysis has opened a new era in the study of sperm behavior. A researcher obtains a sample of sperm from an adult male volunteer. The male must not ejaculate for 3-5 days prior to the visit. Only the truly dedicated are selected. This gives the greatest number of sperm to be observed. It is like waiting for the weekend sex romp. Except in this case, the sex romp is a small room inside a research facility(with adult magazines and a little television playing porn movies). Sparing the slippery details, a sperm sample is "obtained". The donor is paid and sent on his way. The sample is immediately analyzed, usually within 30 minutes. The squiggly batch is placed on a slide under a microscope. Now the computer takes over. A video camera sends an image to a computer. The computer traces each individual sperm path. These paths are plotted and appear as diagrams on a computer screen. This technological breakthrough has allowed scientists to study the swimming patterns of sperm. What they have found is amazing. If the sperm is defective, deformed, or otherwise distorted, it will swim erratically. It is incapable of making the long journey to the egg. No new news there. This could be genetic, or the result of long-term exposure to toxic chemicals. What has also been discovered is that sperm outside the body will swim in a straight line. Sperm react to the chemicals they are immersed in at the time. The female reproductive tract is loaded with chemicals, hormones, and other organic messengers. Once the sperm is exposed to the biochemicals found in a woman's vagina, their group trajectory will widen. They "fan out" like a platoon of Marines on patrol. This allows them to block other sperm from passing them by.

The sperm in the back will actually slow down while the front sperms speed up. The reproductive tract of the female becomes a combat zone. If two males have deposited their sperm in the female, we are looking at a battle of over a billion sperm. Jeesh. Compare that to the Allied invasion of France in World War II. D-Day. D-Day is one of the largest battles that mankind has ever fought. Only three hundred thousand men attacked the beaches. The number of sperm in a single human female is fifty times this after mating with only two men. The reproductive tract inside a female human becomes the front line for a sperm war that takes place over the course of several days. Only one sperm among all of the billions within her reproductive tract can fertilize the egg. Statistically a very small percentage of sperm are even capable of fertilization. This number is estimated to be as low as 1%. That means 99% of the sperm have an entirely different function. Scientists have theorized that these sperm block foreign sperm from fertilizing the egg. They are like the lineman of a football team. No glory for them, but their role is essential for the "star" to score. They make the way for the fastest amongst them to get to the goal. In this case the egg. Blocker sperm take two roles. There may even be two types. The first type of blocker sperm hinder the passage of sperm that enter the female after they do. This is the rear echelon. An invading force must protect the rear. These sperm do just that. The second type of blocker sperm actually attack sperm that have been delivered prior to themselves. These are the expeditionary forces. The Navy S.E.A.L.S. of the spermatozoa set. They seek out and attack, with great vengence, any sperm that are trying to beat them to the egg. This sperm competition is a numbers game. The man with the biggest ejaculate has more sperm to block other males, both front and back. Fertilization through superior firepower. The largest army will win by attrition. Like Mongol hordes razing the countryside, the superior-numbered army will triumph. This has caused the evolution of large testicles. The larger-testicular men produced more sperm. Their traits, including large testicles, are passed on to the next generation. Pretty wild, huh? Take a swig.

The human male may be aware of the inherent unfaithfulness of his mate on a biological level. Baker and Beillis, those tireless sex researchers, have found that the volume of sperm that a man release is not related to how long it has been since he last ejaculated. In other words, if he jacked off two days previous on the flight from New York to Phoenix (qualifying him for the self-service chapter of the Mile High Club), it made no difference in the size of his ejaculate when he met his wife in a hotel room in Phoenix. What actually made the difference in the size of ejaculate was when he last had sex with his wife. The volume of sperm can be three times larger than normal if the man has spent a considerable amount of time away from his wife. Is this an evolutionary strategy developed to combat the inherent wanderings of Cave Harlot? Could it be that the man is simply horny and has a reserve of sperm waiting for his wife? On the other hand, is he sending in reinforcements to the battleground just in case? Like the United States did after World War II? We built military bases all over the world. Let us ponder that it is the subconscious thought of his wife messing around that increases the amount of ejaculate.

Ω

We mentioned that substances in the female reproductive tract affected the behavior of sperm. But what role does the female play in selecting sperm for her own fertilized egg? Baker tells us that the female orgasm plays a logistical role in sperm production. During orgasm, the uterus contracts rhythmically. The contractile action draws sperm into the cervix. This benefits the man that caused her to orgasm. I step gingerly around the penis size debate on this one. One line of thinking is that the longer penis will deposit sperm deeper into the vagina, closer to the cervix. These sperm do not have to swim as far. They are already there. A longer penis will also stimulate the clitoris more due to its length. It rubs with greater surface area per stroke. A thick penis will cause even more friction, leaving the clitoris in a frenzied state. Orgasm will come quicker with the thick penis. It is the long, thick penis that woman say give the best orgasms. (Don't bother asking her, she won't say.) Long and thick may be selected because it is sending the sperm into a better position due to its length, and it is rubbing the clitoris with greater intensity due to its girth. This would cause a more intense orgasm in the female. This orgasm will cause the uterus to rhythmically contract, virtually sucking in all the sperm that was deposited. A point to ponder. But not to worry. After all she chose you. Drink it slow - it's cold.

According to psychologists Steven Gangestad and Randy Thornhill, of the University of New Mexico, women choose different types of men at different stages of their menstrual cycle. Cave Harlot hits all of the bases. Gangestad and Thornhill digitized the faces of men and divided them into categories. They measured various features and assigned them a number. Chin length, jaw length, and other measurements were tallied and faces assigned as either traditionally masculine, traditionally feminine, or somewhere in between. These two fine researchers concluded that women would choose different types of men during different stages of her menstrual cycle. During her most fertile period, most women chose the strong masculine features of the alpha male face. During her infertile period, women would choose men with more feminine characteristics. The implication here supports earlier hypotheses on the strategy of Cave Harlot. Cave Harlot copulates with the strong, masculine alpha male during the time when she would be most likely to conceive; she copulates with the soft, caretaker type when she is not ovulating. The caretaker cuckold thinks the child is his so he sticks around and provides for the newborn. The banks of America are filled with this type of male. They offer a good home, stable environment, and provide well for their family. Did you ever see a chubby coach whose son is the star athlete? Hmmm…

There are dozens of species of primates that practice multi-male reproductive strategies. Dr. Jerry Wolff, of the University of Memphis in Tennessee, studies reproductive behavior in animals. Dr. Wolff has documented multi-male mating in hundreds of species. The primate world, monkeys, marmosets, tamarins, chimpanzees, gorillas, and humans dominate these. Apparently, the multi-male mating strategy has its evolutionary advantages in the primate world. It may be firmly implanted in our female partners to seek attention from other males. The strategy of Cave Harlot may have been passed down to her by "Slutmonkey". From a strictly biological view, this strategy makes perfect sense. If the goal is to perpetuate the species, then the female with the most resources available to her offspring will produce the most children that reach reproductive age. They may see Cave Harlot in action and learn from her. In other words, the female offspring take their cues from their mother and have multiple partners. The male offspring seek out slutty women because their mother was a slut and that is the type of woman which they feel the most comfortable. Save that one for Freud. Either way, the promiscuous primates reproduced at a faster rate than the repressed primates. Sexual repression did not give primates an evolutionary advantage. Sexual promiscuity and the multi-male partnering theory was what gave rise to primate proliferation. In addition, human beings are at the top of that evolutionary mountain. Therefore, it is no stretch of the imagination that the natural order of the female of the species is that of wanton harlot having sex with multiple male partners in order to raise as many well fed, healthy children as possible. These children were taught by multiple males (did you really think he was your uncle?) how to hunt, fish and take advantage of what society has to offer. Let's stop there for a quick chug.

Ω

The multi-male reproductive strategy is interesting. However, if it were so successful in the primate world, would not we see it in other species of animals as well? Well, we do. Dr, Wolff, from the University of Memphis, Tennessee has shown that most mammals use a form of this strategy. From marsupials (kangaroos, wallabies, and the like), to buffalo, field mice, and prairie voles. Yes, prairie voles. They were once thought upon as the paragon of virtue. Prairie voles were believed by scientists to mate for life. If their mate died then the prairie vole would never mate again. Dr. Wolff has disproved this theory with the help of his graduate student, Shawn Thomas. Their research shows that prairie voles do not mate for life as previously assumed. The prairie vole whores around like female primates. The male assumes he is the top vole while his slutty partner is out doing it with every long-tailed, buck-toothed scumbag that has a mouthful of seeds. So much for the myth of the monogamous vole. *Oh, home on the range, where the deer and the prairie vole play....* And speaking of deer. Dr. Wolff has found the same licentious behavior in deer, elk and many other ungulates. It appears that the evolution of mammals was very competitive. Only the strong survived. However, females found a way to survive despite their physical inferiority to males. Darwin's selection of the fittest is a nice theory. But what makes a fit female? Superior strength and hunting ability? Female lions have half of those traits, but not both. No, Darwin was a victim of the sexually repressed times in which he lived. He did not see that it is "Survival of the Sluttiest." Moreover, the sluttiest females attracted the strongest males with their wiles. Cave Harlot was doing just fine up to and including the golden days of the Roman Empire.

Roman mythology is rife with stories of woman being lured to their infidelities by the various gods and demigods. Rome loved it's harlots. That is until the emperor Constantine decided to consolidate power in a divided Rome by pretending to see a vision of Jesus. In a politically motivated act, he united the pagan holidays with the Christian holidays. No one seemed to notice that all of the holidays were at the same time with different names. But that is another story. This marked the inauguration of the influence of Christianity on the actions of Cave Harlot. From those dark days onward, Cave Harlot was relegated to the backs of Chevy's and fraternity parties. There is some indication that there has been a reemergence of Cave Harlot in the last thirty years. That is, if we truly believe that Cave Harlot ever really left. Maybe she just lay dormant throughout history. Hidden to the discerning eye. Painted in the shade of Da Vinci's masterpieces. With the relaxing of restrictions on sexuality it appears that the sexual strategy of Cave Harlot is back in play.

Ω

In the United States DNA testing has come of age. Men no longer rely on the child taking on their characteristics as a paternity test. DNA tests are becoming routine. Men realize that women fool around behind their back. In a recent study by the U.S. Government DNA paternity tests have proven that over 30% of fathers that are paying child support are not the biological father of the child that they are supporting. Gentlemen, the Legend of Cave Harlot lives on. Around 300,000 DNA paternity tests are performed annually. Thirty percent of 300,000 is, for the mathematically challenged, around 90,000 men. Ninety thousand men are paying their ex-wife child support for a child that is not even theirs! In addition, most are doing so unwittingly. They think that the child is theirs; they were told the child is theirs, and they are forced to pay monthly as if the child is theirs. However, the DNA tests are showing that one-third of these poor saps are paying for someone else's child. You ain't the only one that got screwed.

That is the sexual strategy of Cave Harlot. It is alive and well in the 21st century. Despite the thousands of years of religious persecution, Cave Harlot has survived. Sort of like discovering a species of animal that was long thought to be extinct and finding out that they were living amongst us the whole time. But wait! It does not end there. This is an annual survey. The 90,000 men that pay for someone else's successful sperm victory is an annual figure. What does that add up to in the last ten years? Drink up. Dad?

The onslaught of television shows like Desperate Housewives, and Sex in the City are encouraging more women to have extramarital affairs. That 90,000 suckers a year number increases every twelve months. If we take the last ten years as a base for mathematical argument we would see that 900,000 men in America today are paying child support for someone else's child. Exactly the strategy Cave Harlot has used for the last 10,000 years. Multiple males providing for her offspring. Hmmmm. These are just the statistics on child support. What about the hapless fool that is working ten hours a day to put a roof over the head of his ex-wife and someone else's kids? There are over 4,000,000 children born each year in the United States. Using the same percentage for discussion sake would give us 1,200,000 cuckolded fathers victimized by the deceptions of Cave Harlot and her wily ways. The wife stays home; the husband goes out to bring home the bacon. The wife does her cheating while hubby is away. Just like in the cave days. With record numbers of women entering the workforce only the place and time has been changed. A quick hump in the back of the cave is replaced by a quick tryst in the copy room during the office Christmas party. And what happens if the man finds out about this ruse on the part of his female? Would not it constitute fraud? Does she have to pay him back the money he has paid out? Think again, justice seeker. While paternity treachery may be considered a form of fraud, the law provides enough loopholes for Cave Harlot to emerge victorious. When the baby is born, the mother can name anyone she wants as the father. With, or without, his consent. It immediately goes on the birth certificate, a legal document. The male named has only thirty days to dispute his paternity. It does not matter if he is serving in the military or in prison. The law is clear. Thirty days and that is it, aware or not. Think of all the American soldiers named as a father while fighting overseas. After that, he is required to pay child support, or face long, expensive, legal battles to clear his name.

Ω

Now that we think about it, maybe the church was not off the mark after all. The priest that came along and tried to quell this reproductive strategy may have had a point. Some under-hung priest that wanted to possess his women probably started it. Morals needed to be instilled in our young, nubile Cave Harlot. Men around the world agreed. We must keep our women from the larger, more adequate males. However, morality was not enough to overcome the thousands of years of reproductive success. Soldiers, police, and guards became rife with the former alpha males of yesteryear. This may explain the high number of marital affairs that involve police officers and firefighters. Are they the last of the real men? A secret society of super studs that meet women daily? Is there more to the allure of men in uniform? Food for thought. Beer to drink.

Nevertheless, let us go beyond biology. During the late 1960's and into the early 1970's we saw many revolutions in this country. All of our institutions were being examined and dismantled for what they were. One of these many movements was the Women's Liberation Movement. Women were saying that they were second-class citizens because, and only because, men had kept them under their thumb for the last 500 years. Therefore, women burned their bras and came out screaming that they wanted equal rights. They wanted to be afforded all of the opportunities that men had opened to them. There was a minor skirmish and finally men capitulated. Therefore, jobs and careers opened up to women that had previously been "men only". By the late 1970's eager women had invaded just about every male-dominated institution; vigorous women ready to cast off the shackles of 500 years of oppression and prove themselves the better man - to men. Therefore, we all thought that one day society would be marked by a 50-50 mix of men and women surgeons of equal standings, male and female lawyers both on the par of the likes of F. Lee Bailey, chefs of both sexes cooking like Emeril. Except for one simple fact: It never happened. Women have been afforded the open door policy of entering into men's institutions for the last forty years. If women were truly intellectual, and physical, equals to men we would have seen a revolution like no other in the history of the world. The United States of America would have been the template for women achieving equal status throughout the civilized world. Heck, even the Muslims would have had to say,

> "Honestly, Akbar, it appears that wimen is
> eekwills. Oh well, Mohammed was wrong.
> Let us move on. Look at all those successful
> women in the U.S."

Except for one undeniable fact. In the last forty years, women have not become equals to men. In fact, women have become less involved in career fields that have been traditionally male. There are fewer female doctors today, per capita, than in the 1940's. There are fewer female police officers, per capita, today than in the 1930's. Women have increased their numbers in the less cerebral fields like politics. However, in the male-dominated intellectual careers, women have fallen far behind men. Except in one field.

Pornography. Have another sip.

Yes, women have excelled in one field since the "Women's Revolution." And that field is pornography. According to studies by the Restaurant and Bar Managers Association, there has been a 2500% increase in strip joints in the last forty years. The exponential production of adult movies can hardly be measured. What was once a backroom extravagance for seedy bachelors has now become a legitimate industry worth billions of dollars a year. The emergence of Cave Harlot is happening right before our eyes. The yoke of Christian repression has been lifted. Over the last forty years, surveys have indicated that over three-fourths of female porn stars come from "strong religious backgrounds". This seems to signify the re-emergence of Cave Harlot from her repressive Christian vacillations. The true thinking woman of the 21st century knows who she is and wants to follow her loins. Chug-a-lug.

4

Maternal Instinct

Appetizer
Absolut Vodka

Main Course
Sam Adams Summer Ale

Women know how to *get* married- they don't know how to *be* married. In society, as in nature, it is the male that keeps the family together. Maternal instincts are a myth. That doesn't mean women are bad people. It just means that maternal instincts don't exist. Women feel less cerebral loyalty to their children, beyond hormonal maternal care, than do men. And there is a reason or that. A man's security, and his survival, depends on his ability to keep his family intact. Take a big drink here. You may not like some of this. Plus, Sam Adams is a very good ale.

Nature has selected females that choose their own safety and well being over that of their offspring. Why? To be heartless and cruel? No, not at all. Simply because it was necessary for the survival of the species. Maternal infanticide is common. More biological mothers kill their children than do biological fathers. Men have worked together for centuries and have taken loyalty to the level that it is today in most male-dominated societies. Regardless if it is family, a sports team, or a job; men are loyal to their family and peers. Women are not loyal creatures because they do not engage in group endeavors that promote loyalty and teamwork the same way that men do. Loyalty is a learned quality based upon an innate tendency. Women do not possess this innate tendency; nor do they learn this quality as part of their social conditioning. Men routinely perform the supreme sacrifice and die for their families, their ideas, and their country. Women do not possess the capacity for, nor understand, sacrifice. They think sacrifice is staying home with the kids. It is the husband that provides a stable environment for the family while receiving minor benefits from the arrangement. Many men undergo emotional torture to preserve their families. Men sacrifice their health, time and dignity to make a marriage work. And, after all of his acquiescence it is usually the wife that files for divorce. Biologically, women are self-centered creatures and this attribute extends into their destruction of the family in America today. Sorry to inform you, Bubba, but it wasn't your fault.

Maternal instincts are quite uncommon in the animal world. Consequently, they are also rare in human biology or culture. It is a myth, created by males, that the bond between mother and child is one of the strongest bonds in nature. Throughout history, learned men could not understand the ease at which women abandon, injure, or kill their babies. Therefore, the myth of maternal instincts was born. These men hoped that the female would make the self-fulfilling prophecy of maternal instinct a reality. This has worked to a small degree over the centuries. However, like the tale of Oedipus and his mother, it is a myth, designed to teach a value, with no basis in reality. There are two instincts basic to all creatures that have inhabited this planet since "the beginning". These are survival and reproduction. In order for a human female, or the female of any species to survive, they must have the instinct to leave their offspring behind in the face of danger. A female cave dweller could run a lot faster without her baby from the saber-toothed tiger than with it. That same female is spared if the saber-toothed tiger gorges himself on her child and not her. It would be unfair to say that this is the first action a female will take if threatened with danger. But it is a close second.

That is what reality, and scientific research, demonstrates. Nature has selected against woman sacrificing themselves for anyone (or anything). Accordingly, it is instinctual that woman save themselves over their offspring in order to reproduce again and ensure the survival of the species.

Males of various species show quite different behavior than the self-preservation that characterizes their females. It is the male that instinctively protects the offspring of his pack, flock, group, pod, or tribe. Nature selected this instinct for the purpose of sacrificing the individual for the survival of the group-in this case the male is sacrificed. If the male stops the threat, then the pack, flock, group, pod, or tribe will survive. If the male is killed in the attack, his offspring will survive beyond him, taken care of by his female and the other males in the group. You see this "uncle" behavior in human males quite frequently. "The boy needs a man in his life" is a common phrase amongst men and most men will go out of their way to care for a child that is not their own when the child's father is not in the picture. It is classic male behavior. This behavior is absent in females. When was the last time you heard a female going out of her way to set a good example, or spend time with children that were not her own? It is a very atypical behavior amongst human females. Sacrificing the male actually increases the survival rate of the species by allowing more offspring to survive. Natural selection is a brutal, yet effective, process. So what we see as a "selfish, self-serving behavior" is what nature calls "reproductive success".

The instinct for survival in females overrides the maternal care of their children. Therefore, from a biological viewpoint, maternal instinct is a myth - it does not exist. That is not to say that there is no maternal care in a majority of the Earth's organisms. Human mothers do take care of their children. They show maternal care. Without maternal care, most of us would have died of starvation, exposure, or some other environmental malady. Maternal care is what has allowed each species to procreate with great success. However, maternal care is driven solely by hormones and does not extend past the age in which the children are old enough to fend for themselves. This is why most divorces take place "when the kids are old enough." It is the effect of the female human losing her maternal hormones and wanting to push her children out of the nest. When this biologically based behavior is coupled with a society that is sex-obsessed and fearfully tolerant of woman and their insecure sexual needs, we have a recipe for family disaster. That divorce is on the rise is hard to dispute. This is why it is the husband that holds the family together. Imbibe, my reader, imbibe.

Ω

Maternal instinct is absent in human primates, never having to be evolutionarily selected because the temporary natal hormones circulating in the mother were sufficient to keep the offspring alive until it could fend for itself. Nature does not do any more work, or create any systems that it does not need. If the transitory hormonal method of child rearing is sufficient, then that is all the organism will need to survive long enough to reproduce its own offspring and continue the cycle of life. Examples of maternal instinct are hard to find in the natural world. The paternal instinct of species from fish to baboons is what keeps the young protected. It is the behavioral instincts of the male that propagates the young and keeps the cycle of life going. Research with many fish species shows that the male builds the nest, cares for the young, attracts the female with his ornate coloring; and/or elaborate mating dance, and is more protective of the small fry for a longer time. The female usually lays the eggs and leaves. There are no instincts to keep her around. This is seen in seahorses. The male impregnates the females and then takes the embryos into his own brood sac after they are fertilized. He keeps them in his brood sac until they are fully developed and then cares for them when they are born. The male seahorse is the one that gives birth. If the female is around she will eat the young along with any other food she happens to find. No maternal instinct there. And, since there are no hormones to regulate her behavior, the female seahorse does not discern between her own child and a delicious floating planktonic morsel when it comes to dinner time. Other organisms behave the same.

Remember when you were a kid and you found a bird's nest with eggs in it? Everyone told you not to touch it or the mother would abandon the eggs. The simple act of touching the eggs allows the female to act on her strong survival instincts and leave her future children to cool down and die. Birds make great examples of instinctual behavior. Take the cuckoo bird. The cuckoo is a grayish, visually plain bird with a slim body, long tail and strong legs. The majority of Cuckoos dine primarily on caterpillars, which are distasteful to other birds. There are many species of cuckoo, with most practicing the sexual strategy of egg parasitism. The Common Cuckoo (Cuculus canorus) is a member of the order of birds called Cuculioformes. The breeding habitat for the cuckoo contains open fields with reed beds and trees around the edges. In the reed bed another species of bird, the Reed Warbler, makes its nest. The female Cuckoo will spend a long time watching over the reed beds in their neighborhood. Like a thief casing the joint, the female cuckoo is spying on the movements and actions of the Reed Warbler female. The hapless male Cuckoo has no idea what his lovely wife is up to. He thinks she is going to stay at home and raise his feathered progeny herself. Another trusting male believing that his mate has the best interests of the family in mind. Female deception is very common in the animal world. Anyway, the female Cuckoo is watching the happy, unaware, warbler family. Cuckoo mama knows that the warbler will have to leave her nest to gather food. It is not known how Cuckoo mama knows exactly when to swoop down to the warbler nest – but she does. She glides in on silent air, pushes one of the warbler eggs out of the nest (to its death on the ground below), and lays her own egg in its place. Then she flies off cackling a sound that tiptoes the border between laughter and hysterical crying. The warbler returns and does not notice that a much larger egg is in her nest. She sits on all the eggs until they hatch. After hatching the Cuckoo chick grows much larger than the warbler chicks. At 14 days old the Cuckoo chick (cuckoo chick? I know a few of them, don't you?) is three times the size of his adopted brothers and sisters. Its tireless screams stimulate the adoptive parents to bring more food, which it consumes voraciously. The other chicks do not stand a chance. But starving isn't fast enough for the invader. The Cuckoo chick pushes the Warbler chicks out of the nest by rolling them with its back over the walls of the nest. And what does the warbler mother-to-be do while her future progeny are being pushed to their death? She sits on a nearby branch and watches, doing nothing to stop the carnage. Maternal instincts are a myth.

Have you heard the myth of the female lion? In brief it says that the lioness is the pillar of strength that keeps the pride of lions stable. Sorry, Charlie, but another folk tale bites the dust. Lioness's show no maternal instinct beyond that which is regulated by the hormones of parturition and suckling. If the Alpha male lion (the father of her children) is killed in battle, it is his adversary that takes over the pride. According to researcher Craig Packer, distinguished McKnight University Professor and leading expert on lion behavior, it is the habit of the victorious male to kill all the juvenile offspring of the previous lion king (no wonder Simba left the pride after Scar arranged the murder of Mufasa). This assures that the females will be receptive to him to bear his cubs. This is a cruel example of survival of the fittest. The strongest male lives to produce his line of cubs, the weaker males' offspring are killed off. You may not agree with this strategy but it is the law of the jungle. What does the fierce lioness do while her children are being slaughtered by the new king? Nothing. She just lays there until they are all dead. Then she does something. And it isn't extract revenge with the help of her sisters. No sir. She goes into heat and has sex with the new king a dozen times a day until she is pregnant. Not just one of them; the whole slut pride squats down and gets a royal humping by the new lion king. This says something about the virility of the male lion, but it speaks volumes about the lack of loyalty on the lioness' part. She shows no loyalty to her old suitor by helping him fight off the intruder. She shows no loyalty to her own children as they are mercilessly exterminated amidst their anguished cries for help. She shows loyalty only to herself as she spreads her ass and gets repeatedly ridden like a drunken hooker on an aircraft carrier full of sailors. This behavior is so common in other animals it has its own name. It is called the Bruce Effect.

The Bruce Effect, named after Hilda Bruce, is when a pregnancy terminates in mammals due to the presence, or smell, of a strange male that is not the biological father of the fetus. The Bruce Effect is observed in twelve species of rodents. The female terminates her pregnancy and then mates with the new male- allegedly to avoid infanticide after parturition. The same effect is found in primates. The female undergoes a series of biochemical changes that result in the abortion of her unborn fetuses. Maternal instincts, if present, would not allow this infanticide to take place. Maternal instincts would override the behavior of the female. That is, if maternal instincts did exist.

We could continue to explore maternal instincts in nature and not find any examples worthy of investigation. And they certainly do not appear in human females, either biologically or culturally. It is culture that gives humans the edge over animals. We have rituals that keep our animal instincts subdued while the greater good of the group can be enhanced. It is our culture that has allowed men to flourish and keep women from doing excessive damage to their families. But culture is not always enough. As we have seen before—women are not loyal beings. They have evolved to take care of themselves before all others. The number of women that abuse their children supports this finding.

It is no secret that woman are abusive to their children. Most children suffer their first form of physical abuse from their mothers. Women abuse their children at rates much higher than men. This is confirmed by quite a few major studies on child abuse in this country. Mothers in America do not simply slap their children for misbehavior. They go beyond the physical abuse by neglecting their children's needs, inflicting psychologically abuse, sexual abuse and emotional abuse on their children far more often than any other family member. In a compilation of child abuse incidents from the National Child Abuse and Neglect Data System, the following statistics were recorded. But you knew this already, right?

Type of Abuse	Fathers	Mothers
Physical Abuse	46%	54%
Neglect	25%	75%
Medical Neglect	18%	82%
Psychological Abuse	47%	53%
Fatalities	33%	67%

These statistics speak for themselves, with reported incidents of physical abuse women outpacing men by 8% nationwide. You see a similar trend with psychological abuse.

What separates men and women is the neglect and the fatalities. Women are three times more likely to neglect their children than men. In addition, this is only what is being reported. The real situation is probably more dismal. In medical neglect the gap is even wider. Women are four times more likely to ignore their sick children than men are. So much for maternal instinct. The real eye-opener is when the abuse leads to the death of the child. Women are three times as likely to kill their children as men. At least she didn't do that.

When was the last time you heard of a man killing his children? The only incident that comes to memory at all was John List in the 1970's. If you watch the news you get inundated with child-killers like Susan Smith, Andrea Yates, Amy Grossberg, Melissa Drexsler, Christina Riggs, Casey Anthony and a plethora of others. All are "average" women who just happened to snuff out the life of their own children. The majority of these defenseless babies were slaughtered for the selfish personal reasons of their mothers. They wanted to start fresh, without the encumbrance of children. Sound self serving? Take Susan Smith, for example. Feeling no loyalty to her children, or her husband, she strapped her babies in their car seats and pushed the car into a lake. She lied on national television for weeks. Cried crocodile tears. What a horror.

Then there's the shocking case of Mary Beth Tinning of Schenectady, New York. Between 1949 and 1968, Tinning had 10 children -7 girls and 3 boys. Not one lived to see a second birthday. Two of the children died within a month. One of her babies died after thirteen days, another after 14 months. Tinning reported that the babies had died in their sleep. All babies were home alone with Tinning when they died. It took decades before Tinning finally admitted, at age seventy, that she smothered each baby to death. Maternal instincts? Time for a shot.

Thousands of babies are abandoned each year in the United States alone. These go far beyond the homeless mother selflessly leaving her baby on the doorstep of a rich family so that it can have a better life. Most are discarded, as you would throw away a pair of shoes - in dumpsters, down wells, shallow graves, and other convenient methods of disposal. Take the case of eighteen-year-old Melissa Drexsler. Melissa arrived at her prom, went to the restroom, and gave birth to a baby boy. The baby died and Melissa left his body in a garbage can. After straightening herself up, Melissa Drexsler returned to the dance floor to enjoy the rest of her prom. Her powers of recuperation were only eclipsed by her extreme shortage of compassion towards her own child. These examples of a lack of devotion bring home the fact that women do not feel loyalty to their family, only to themselves. This lack of loyalty is unleashed when the female finally has extracted every bit of humanity from her husband that she can and divorces him for her own selfish reasons of pursuing other men. Like I said. Bubba, it wasn't anything you did. Take a big swallow.

Ω

Men believe in their families. They think rationally and see the significance of their role in raising children. Men see the importance of providing a stable home life for their offspring. And how does American society repay the male of the species for his dedication? By making divorce so lucrative to his wife he must beg her daily just to stay in the house; never mind treat him with decency and respect. He endures name calling, rejection of every sort, taunting, teasing, physical abuse, neglect, and on and on. But still, it is the male that keeps the family together, even under the most difficult conditions. And many males know how difficult some women can be to live with.

If you are divorced you tried to maintain your families' security while enduring emotionally painful conditions. The male human being has an instinctual drive to sacrifice himself for the good of his clan. It is not a passing hormonal phase. But even if it were hormonal, it would be that wonderful male hormone - testosterone, the male sex hormone. Testosterone drives male behavior to an extent that is not quite understood by science. If testosterone drives a man's lifelong loyalty to his family that would explain why men never cease in the protection of their family. This hormone stays with a man until the day he dies, as does the instinct to protect his family. Hormone, or instinct, the end result is the same. In women the hormones are transitory, cyclical, and rapidly diminish to insignificant levels after menopause. More on female hormones in a later chapter.

The most solid, measurable indicator of marital discord in a society is divorce. This is the step that two people, who at one time thought that their souls were joined in another astral plane, that believed they were meant to spend the rest of their life with this person out of the six billion others by divine Providence, after having pledged their undying love and devotion to one another till death do us part, say:

"Screw this! I'm outta here."

There are a variety of factors that lead to this breakup of the family. There have been many studies, books, articles, theses papers and opinions as to why people divorce. That is another subject for another time. What needs to be looked at is who is divorcing whom. Which member of the marriage is giving up and condemning the children to a life of "coming from a broken home." Is it the husband or the wife? According to a recent study by the British Broadcasting Company, the female Homo sapiens files for divorce in 93% of the divorces in the United Kingdom. The rate is only slightly lower in the United States and Canada. Ninety-three percent. Roughly speaking, in 9 out of ten divorces, it is the woman that is filing for a legal document to destroy the home of the children and their emotional security. That is a very significant number. The United States sees a similar trend amongst its married couples. In more than three-fourths of the divorce cases it is the American female that files for divorce. Even in Canada, known for its progressive trends, the wife is responsible for the destruction of the family 70 % of the time. And the reason? What most woman cite that they are "just not happy" in the marriage. They leave their family, shatter the security of their children, cause long term emotional damage to these same children, make the financial situation worse for everyone involved, and physically divide the family along parental lines. All because the female is only concerned with her own happiness.

It is up to the husband, the father, to keep the family together. Men realize in the beginning of the marriage that this embittered lifestyle is not what they had envisioned when they said "I do". Very early in the marriage many men realize that they have made a drastic mistake. They watch the woman that they married change into a modified version of their mother-in-law. She gains weight, cuts her hair short, changes from thongs to cotton briefs (with the reinforced crotch). Eww. Drink. Drink. Drink.

Men are team players. They do the best they can to hold the family together. Especially if there are children involved. Even under the worst of conditions. And no one can make conditions worse for a man than the American female. "Marry in hast, repent in leisure", says Ben Franklin. When you hear people describe a marriage in uneven terms you usually hear that it is the husband that is put upon.

"She's a nag." (There is no male equivalent for this phrase.)

"He's hen-picked." (There is no male equivalent for this phrase.)

"She keeps a messy house". (He's a slob.)

"She let herself go after the second child." (He's a slob.)

"He gives her everything, and she still wants more. (There is no male equivalent for this phrase.)

"She's high maintenance." (Definitely no male equivalent for this phrase.)

Yes, it is the male Homo sapiens that endures the most unbearable conditions in marriage. And what does the man benefit? It is not emotional support. No, it isn't a massive stroking of his ego. A nightly massage? Yeah, right. Nor do men benefit financially from a marriage (quite the contrary). It is usually not a sexually adventurous relationship for the man. The sexual interest level wanes after a few years (months? weeks? days?). This is why there is such a high rate of infidelity in marriages. Is it companionship? Fear of being alone? Why do men get married if there is no benefit for them in the marriage? Are men just there to bring in the prestige and money that allows their children to thrive in society? Is it his role to provide for his family without receiving anything back from them? It is like the classic recipe for cooking frogs. If you drop a frog into hot water it will jump out. But if you place a frog in warm water and gradually turn up the temperature the frog will stay there until he is cooked. That is the way that women hook men into families. They show no indication of their future intentions (warm water) before marriage. If they did show their beau their future behavior he would react like the frog that jumped out of the hot water. By the time the man, like the frog, realizes that he is screwed it is too late. Let's delve into this lopsided relationship.

It appears that the man of the house is responsible for a lot more than bringing in the money. In the book, Marriage: The Safest Place for Women and Children, by Patrick

Fagan and Kirk Johnson, Ph.D., Dr. Johnson established that the situation that most effectively protects mothers and children from domestic abuse and violent crime is marriage. A summary of the findings of the National Crime Victimization Survey, which the U.S. Department of Justice has conducted annually since 1973, demonstrates that mothers who are married are far less likely to suffer from violent crime than are mothers who are not married. You did you best, she just screwed you over.

Reports of domestic abuse come from women that are not married more than women that are married. The incidence of boyfriend, or "unwed domestic partner", abuse is twice as high among single mothers who have never been married as it is among mothers who are married to the father of their children. And the same report shows that married women endure far less violent crime than single women. The National Crime Victimization Survey compiles its statistics on victimization through yearly surveys of American citizens. In this survey violent crime is defined as rape, sexual assault, robbery, aggravated assault, and simple assault. The really nasty stuff that hurts people physically and emotionally. Domestic abuse is defined as violent crimes from someone that lives in the house, or is intimately connected to the victim. These include a spouse, former spouse, boyfriend/girlfriend, former boyfriend/girlfriend, son, daughter, grandma, grandpa, aunts, uncles, and other relatives. Mothers of young children that have never married are three times more likely to be victims of violent crime than are mothers who are married. These figures include mothers that are single and living alone, with a boyfriend, or are "shacking up" with the alleged biological father of their child. Children from a broken home, or from mothers that have never married, are at greater risk. The National Crime Victimization Survey has reported that these children are thirty times more likely to suffer abuse than the child that is with his married biological parents. *Thirty times*. These unfortunates are thirty times more likely to suffer from child abuse from than from children raised by both biological parents in marriage. Your ex-wife will place your children in an environment in which they are thirty times more likely to be abused. Remember the lioness?

Sometimes the abuse gets very severe. Children have been killed after years of abuse. When an abused child dies, the correlation between previous abuse and family structure jump off the page. The rate of children killed in step-families is three times higher than the biological married parents. It jumps up to nine times higher in the single mom scenario, eighteen times higher in the cohabiting but not married family, and rises exponentially to seventy-three times higher where mother cohabits with a boyfriend that is not the father of the child. *Seventy-three times higher.* Are you kidding me? You did your best. This could be anyone, not exclusively the mother or new boyfriend. If your ex-wife brings your children into an environment where she is living with her boyfriend, the chances of them being killed skyrockets to seventy-three times the norm. The Drinking Man knows this. It is instinctual knowledge to male human beings that they will protect their own children better than anyone else. It is a stressful event when a biological father has lost his children in a divorce. Intuitively he knows that he has truly lost them. It becomes unbearable when a boyfriend comes into the picture. There is hardly an American male in this country that does not know of a case of the boyfriend of the ex-wife being abusive to her children. The abuse may be mild - neglect, rudeness, cold and distant attitude. It usually turns to something more confrontational- pushing, shoving, intimidation and threats. And it can turn to severe abuse - emotional, physical, and sexual. It may also lead to the death of the child seventy-three times more often than if the biological parents had stayed together.

Moreover, what becomes of the young girls that have their biological fathers in the home? Dr. Meb Meeker, in her book, *Strong Fathers, Strong Daughters*, lists the benefits of young girls that have their biological father present in their home.

-toddlers securely attached to fathers are better at solving problems.

-six-month-old babies score higher on tests of mental development if their dads are involved in their lives.

-with dads present in the home, kids manage stress better.

-girls whose fathers provide warmth and control achieve higher academic success.

-Girls who are close to their fathers exhibit less anxiety and withdrawn behaviors.

-parent connectedness is the number one factor in preventing girls from engaging in premarital sex and indulging in drugs and alcohol.

-girls with doting fathers are more assertive.

-daughters who feel connected to their fathers have significantly fewer suicide attempts, fewer instances of body dissatisfaction, depression, low self–esteem, and unhealthy weight.

-girls with involved fathers are twice as likely to stay in school.

-daughters' self-esteem is best predicted by her father's physical affection.

And in the absence of the father? The numbers of stepfathers that are having sexual relationships with their stepdaughters is underreported. Many young women suffer irreparable emotional damage at a crucial developmental stage due to the selfishness of the mother, and her new boyfriend. Most young victims report sexual abuse to their mothers. And, in true female fashion, the mother's choose survival-their daughter's accusations fall on deaf ears. The mother sometimes blames the daughter. Sexual abuse of a child is rampant where the mother has taken her daughters to live with a "new" male.

The numbers increase when violent crime outside the house is taken into account. If the woman was married she is suffering violent crime at a rate of 52 crimes per 1000 mothers. The never-married mother is experiencing crime at almost three times this rate, or 149 violent crimes per 1000 mothers. This could be explained as simply that a woman alone in our society is a target for every predator that sees her. The presence of a married biological father in the family cuts this statistic in half. Could it be that our grandparents and forebears were not simply prudish on their ideas of monogamy and marriage- but practical? We tend to think of any generation prior to the sexual revolution of the 1960's as "square" and out of touch with their needs as humans. It might be time to rethink these perceptions as the society that we live in today crumbles from the inside out. It is the institution of a male dominated marriage that has made this a great country. Is it so hard to see that the moral degradation of the country is correlated to the dissolution of the family? That is a good question to ponder. It is a great question to bring up at your next boring social event. Step into a group of people discussing some mundane topic and state:

> "Is it so hard to see that the moral degradation of
> the country, mainly perpetuated by females, is
> correlated to the dissolution of the family?"

And wait for an answer. You, having read this book will be able to foster the conversation in the direction that is most advantageous to your hypothesis. Regardless of what happens, the conversation will no longer be boring. But let us not diverge into trivial social conversations. The facts remain that while marriage may not benefit the male of the species very much it appears that marriage is the safest place for a mother and her children to live. The liberated, "I can live quite well without men" women that leave this protective environment, for whatever reason, do so to the detriment of their children's, and their own, safety.

Maureen Dowd, a fairly successful author, has written a book questioning whether men are necessary. The book is even titled, *Are Men Necessary*? Ms. Dowd regurgitates the feminist dogma that the male of the species is not essential to the survival of our kind. Take a look at the statistics, Ms. Dowd. The Drinking Man has to answer the question that you have posed. Yes, Maureen Dowd, Men Are Necessary. Where was your father? The woman that stays married to the biological father of her children will suffer less violent crime than the woman that conceives out of wedlock, or gets divorced. Women that divorce do so at the expense of their children's well-being.

Ω

In *The Unexpected Legacy of Divorce*, author Judith S. Wallerstein, with the help of Julia M. Lewis, and Sandra Blakeslee, sheds light on the emotional effect that divorce has on children. Wallerstein compares children of divorced parents with children from parents that did not divorce. The study takes place over a twenty-five year period. Each person was interviewed many times during the course of their childhood, adolescence, and adult life over the twenty-five years in which the study took place. The results show that divorce has a devastating impact on children. How many times have you heard the female that is initiating divorce say, "It's better for the children this way? Now they won't have to hear us fighting and arguing." Well it appears that that statement is very far from the truth. In reality, in Ms. Wallerstein's study it was found that children do not connect divorce and arguing. They connect the divorce with something they, the children, did. Sure they hope that the arguing would stop. Who wouldn't? But the rational explanation of the selfish mother that applies for divorce in a majority of cases falls on deaf ears. The children do not see the dissolution of their family as being any better than being in a family that is dysfunctional.

For the female, divorce is a way for her to release herself from the responsibilities of the family. She is then free to get a boob job, join a gym, color her hair and go out to see if she "still has it". In the alcohol-reduced pickings of a nightclub, she will not have to try hard to see if she "still has it". As a matter of fact, she will probably "get it" on her first night out. A young buck, full of testosterone, will tell her how beautiful she is, how special she is, and "ba da boom ba da bing". She falls for the line and gets nailed. Sorry, dude, I know that hurts. Believe me, I know. Drink the rest of the beer. Slowly. Enjoy. It wasn't your fault.

She will have all of her needs met, her insecurities appeased, and reinforce that it was her husband that was holding her back. The problem is – her kids won't see it that way. She is escaping a bad relationship. A relationship that went bad because of her inability to communicate her feelings. A relationship that went bad because of her inability to get in touch with her feelings. So she blames her husband, tears the family apart, and out she goes. She is free from her "oppressive" husband.

For her children, her "new beginning" is a tragic ending to the secure, predictable family structure that they know. It is an abrupt end to their childhood. Even if it is dysfunctional, to the kids it is all that they know. They are now forced into their parent's divorce and all of the fun things that goes with the devastating dissolution of their family. From this point forward, every developmental stage will be marked with the parent's divorce.

Birthdays. Divorce.
First Communion. Divorce.
Bar Mitzvah. Divorce.
First dance. Divorce.

First kiss. Divorce.
Summers. Divorce.
Weekends. Divorce.
Holidays. Divorce.
Christmas. Divorce.
Spring Break. Divorce.
High School Prom. Divorce.
The Child's Wedding day. Divorce.
The Birth of the Grandchildren. Divorce.

The divorce of the parents becomes the child's misery at every major occasion that should define a happy childhood, adolescence and adulthood. The absence of the family unit overrides the experience. The family that should be sharing these joyous occasions is not there. The joyous occasion has been tainted by the selfish desire of the female of the species to please herself. The divorce also left the kids without role models as to how to have a good relationship. How to work through problems. The depressed and alienated children of divorce became the depressed and alienated adults of divorce. They were described by Wallerstein as "lacking critical life skills, unable to cope with change, unable to sustain long-term relationships, and unable to communicate their desires, feelings, and needs." Wallerstein points out that children who grow up in dysfunctional families relationships fare better than children of divorce because they feel secure, wanted, and have a role in the family. That role may be one of dysfunction mediator, but it is a role nonetheless. They have not been abandoned. The basic human desire to belong is not extinguished. The only thing worse than feeling pain is feeling nothing. As these children become adults, they will experience higher levels of negative coping behaviors like smoking, drug and alcohol abuse, and eating disorders. These children from broken homes become "workaholics", "sexaholics", and "alcoholics" in order to cope with the fear, pain, anger, and frustration they feel daily. They can't sleep. They chronically overspend. Accumulate debt faster than their peers from intact families. They become compulsive gamblers. They experience chronic depression at higher rates than their peers from intact families. And they seem to want to end their pain through suicide at a higher rate than people from intact families.

Suicide.

A study by the National Institute for Healthcare Research in Rockville, Maryland, indicates that divorce plays a major role in people that commit suicide. The Institute declares that divorce is the number one factor linked with suicide rates in major U.S. cities, well above all other physical, financial, and psychological factors. The World Health Organization has similar findings. In a study of major European cities only one factor could be linked directly to suicide. The World Health Organization found that divorce was the only factor connected statistically with suicide in every one of the major cities. The study showed that factors like poverty, joblessness, and physical disability were loosely associated with a minority of suicides. However, the positive link in all of the cities was the destruction of the family unit – divorce. Divorce initiated by the woman in 90 per cent of the cases. Divorce that is opposed by the husband, as he knows what will happen to his beloved children. But divorce is not the only form of abuse that women broadcast upon their children. The husband keeps the wife from abusing the children in a multitude of selfless ways. And how does society repay the male human being for his undying loyalty to family? By making him look like an inept, nonsexual asshole.

Have you watched any television commercials lately? When husbands are portrayed in television commercials it is usually done by showing the man as a totally inept, bumbling idiot. More so, it is usually white males that are depicted as blundering, overweight losers that cannot get out of their own way. The wife and the children appear to tolerate this balding oaf, who is just not tuned into what is going on in the real world. To watch network television one cannot miss a night where the man of the house is seen as a buffoon. This is usually done to appeal to women to buy the product that is being sold. Even the children know more than dad does. There is a mixed message here; the house is usually spacious and well furnished. The mother doesn't normally work in these commercials, and the man is normally a white male between the ages of thirty and forty. The negative image of men is not limited to television commercials.

In a study performed by James McNamara, of the University of Western Sydney, the results would make even the most ardent conspiracy theorists raise an eyebrow. McNamara analyzed over 650 newspapers, 130 magazines, 125 television news bulletins, 147 television current affairs programs, 125 talk show episodes, and 108 television lifestyle episodes and other media over a 25 week period. He found representations of men in 1,568 newspaper and magazine articles and 231 television reports or program segments. McNamara found that men are overwhelmingly portrayed in a negative fashion in the news media. A breakdown of the statistics shows that 69% of the men depicted in the news are shown in an unfavorable light, compared with 12% favorable, and 19 % of the reports being viewed as neutral towards men. Add that up and you get 88% of the images of men in the media are not favorable. No wonder men have such a hard time keeping their family together. The men were shown to be villains, aggressors, perverts, or totally incompetent at being fathers and husbands. Only a small percentage depicted the man as being a good father, protector, hero, leader, or good husband. This is how society says "Thank you" for being the protector of the family and promoter of our culture into the next generation. No wonder Maureen Dowd thinks men are unnecessary.

The Drinking Man knows that these attitudes contribute to the breakup of the family. Due to her nature, a female human being can never be happy. When this innate misery spills over into the family, it is catastrophic. Everyone in the family suffers in the event of a divorce. Except for one person. The only individual that enjoys a better standard of living after the divorce is the ex-wife/mother. The children and the husband all experience a lowered standard of living, emotional pain, and less financial privileges. Mommy dearest flourishes. And what are the results of this broken family? Single-mother broken families are the vehicle in which children travel to teen pregnancy, high school dropouts, drug abuse, juvenile crime, and even rape. More than eighty percent of males that are in jail for rape come from broken homes. In violent crime, the figure is even higher. Why do women leave the family unit in such disarray? Is it simply to pursue their own interests? Maybe they were never taught to put the needs of others above themselves. Maybe they are just the hapless victims of evolution. Or maybe our society has encouraged women to destroy the family by making it more lucrative and exciting to be divorced than to be married. Could our society have weakened to the point where we allow the weakness of a women's selfish biological nature to ruin our families? Or maybe we have actually believed the seventies bullshit that women were team players because they could play softball on a men's team.

Ω

Teamwork. From the day young boys enter into their first T-ball game it is drilled into their head. Teamwork. We are all part of a team. What is best for the team? We are all here to benefit the team. If the team wins, we win. GO TEAM. Sadly enough, women are not given this training. From Little League sports to warfare, women are not team players. Since the 1970's federal legislation has given young girls the opportunity to compete in the same sports as young boys. Yet, in these forty years the idea of team-work just has not become a part of the female psyche.

I will begin with a story from my coaching days. It was in the mid 1980's when I was first asked to coach a girl's team. I had been coaching a variety of sports for years, basketball, football, track and cross-country. However, I had never coached a girl's team. So it came to happen that I was offered a lucrative position as the head coach of the boy's basketball team at a very reputable middle school. Upon interviewing for the job I was told that there was one catch - I also had to coach girls' soccer team since they could not find a coach. I capitulated with the greater good in mind. What a disaster. Leaving the empty boys' locker room (alone), I encountered a group of young females wearing gym clothes on the soccer field. I introduced my-self as their new coach and requested that everyone take a lap around the perimeter of the field. I was used to boys taking off so they could be the first one back to impress the new coach. Four girls started running and the others started to mill around and walk in the direction of the fabled four. When I repeated my request I was met with a cacophony of cries, "Do we have to?", and "I don't want to get sweaty", and the best one, "My new sneakers will get all dirty." With this brief, yet brutal, introduction I entered into the strangest sports season of my life. These girls were not concerned about the team, but more so how they looked on the team. It was a struggle to simply assign positions. I mis-takenly thought that I just had an inexperienced team so I came up with some team builder activities. What a flop that was. I struggled harder than ever before to build my team and get them ready for the first game. We went into the game in a manner that has since caused me to swear that I would never coach girl's sports again. Having coached football, I know that the first game is very nerve-wracking to the players. They really haven't been tested yet. They do not know where they stand as far as the other teams are concerned. Even veteran teams feel this angst. So until the whistle sounds to start the game the players usually size each other up. They watch the other team shoot, dribble, kick, pass, catch, or whatever warm-ups they can glean some information from. In football I would hear,

> "They don't look so big." or
> "Man, they can't catch." or
> "Watch out for number 34, he looks like
> he is quick."

Not so with the female soccer team I coached. When the other team took the field I heard,

> "Oh, look at her hair." and
> "She is way too big for that outfit." and
> "Do my shin guards look okay? I mean, do
> they match my wrist bands?"

Needless to say, I was deflated. Upon taking the field we did okay,(since the other team was the same species!) with the other team scoring only two goals to our one. At the half, I tried to energize the girls into playing like a team. I failed; all they could talk about was the interpersonal relationships on the field. When I asked what was happening on the field, I heard:

> "Number 23 was mean."
> "Number 45, the one with the thick ankles,
> smells like garlic." (Followed by laughter)
> "Did you see the goalie, she thinks she's hot
> stuff." (She was pretty good looking)

Attempting to interrupt, I tried to rephrase my question as to what was happening strategically on the field that we could adapt to and change. They met me with blank stares.

There was an awkward silence and then they chattered about the other girl's hair and who was too pushy, and a myriad of other non-strategic topics. It was a long season but we actually won a couple of games (I have no idea how!).

That was my only foray into coaching female sports. I just simply could not elevate the females to the level of team play necessary to have a cohesive group working towards the same goal. Every game the topic would usually meander back to the interpersonal relationships between the girls themselves, or the other team. Soccer was ancillary to what was happening on the field. I know that if hell is the compendium of one's fears incarnate; I will be coaching girls' soccer for all eternity with hair spray in one hand and Midol in the other, shouting, "Teamwork! Teamwork!" to echo through the labyrinth of Hell's inner caverns and ante-rooms. So much for coaching female sports. The female homo sapiens are as far from being team players as Karl Marx is from being a CEO for Dow Chemical. Pass me the beer.

Ω

It was after this horrible experience that I started to wonder about the equality of the sexes. During the sixties and seventies all youths were subjected to the rhetoric that girls and boys were equal. That girls could do anything that boys could do. I remembered from my days in the military that the few females we had were never there when the difficult training took place. It was in the late seventies, the time of "everyone's equal", and I was an enlisted man in the U.S. Marine Corps. There is no finer group of loyal human beings than that you will be honored enough to know than the U.S. Marines. Marines pledge to die for each other and the Corps. And they do. Our country is what it is today due mainly to the sacrifices of the U.S. Marine Corps. EWRAH!

But it was also in the Marine Corps that I realized that women were not team players. Whenever there was a long hike, the female Marines (all of them) would be notoriously absent. Sent off to sickbay for toe fungus, cramps, or bloating. Meanwhile the real Marines would be in the field, up to their ass in mud, eating C-rations that were left over from the Korean War. Yet these same females wanted to be treated like Marines, respected like Marines, and given all the authority and respect a male Marine was afforded. I even wrote a letter to the editor of the military monthly newspaper "Stars and Stripes" detailing the lack of teamwork women Marines exhibit, and the unfair advantages that were given to females in the post-Vietnam military. It was published! The females were hopping mad at the truth of that letter for months. I accepted that women were not team players. It was not instilled in them at a young age. Teamwork was not part of what makes a female function. It may even be the breakdown of teamwork that makes women thrives.

Men work together. It is the only way that civilization has evolved to the stage it is in today. We have space exploration, deep ocean exploration, discoveries on the atomic level, and breakthroughs in medicine everyday – all attributed to the teamwork of the male human. This teamwork was evident when Apollo 13 was crippled. The men of NASA pulled together, put egos aside, and brought the spacecraft safely back to Earth. Could you imagine if women were running Mission Control? It would be two days for them just to form a committee to see who would bring snacks! There are many adventures throughout history in which the teamwork of men has propelled them through impossible situations.

The lack of teamwork on the female human being's part is puzzling to the average male. It is usually the female that puts her needs before the families. In America, it is the wife that files for the majority of divorces in America. Men see the family as a team. And even though they realize that maybe their wife is a fat pain in the ass, they stick it out for the sake of the team. Women possess no such loyalties. After years of picking their husband to death over every little thing he does they realize they have nothing left to complain about. So they need a new man to start picking apart. Some poor sap that thinks, "Hey, maybe this girl is different!" She may prevaricate when he asks about why she is still single. Leading him to believe that she is the hapless victim of poor relationships that incidentally were all the fault of a selfish, insensitive man. She tries to make him feel that he is different. *"Climb upon your white horse, my hero, and save me from , uh, this horrible life."*

Ah, but little does he know. The poor sap has been targeted for character assassination. It will only be a matter of hours after the first date when the intelligence on him is being disseminated to her circle of insiders. His job, his height, hairstyle, dating history, bad habits, prospects for enmeshment and the eventual dehydration of his every dream. And that is only the beginning. As each new piece of information is gleaned about his life her girlfriends become more knowledgeable. He has a committee of women that know more about him than he does himself, because his new "friend" has embellished most of it. From this point it is open season. Our male, tempered by years of loyalty and teamwork, thinks that this new "friend" is also a loyal team player. That is where most men make their mistake in a relationship with a woman. They think that women are loyal team players. Some are. But these rare individuals were usually the only girl in a family of boys. They were immersed in teamwork and loyalty and it swelled their personality to tolerable levels. They are the exception, rather than the rule. The majority of women feel no such loyalty.

As the relationship progresses our poor sap is "packaged and sold" to her new girlfriends more and more. If the relationship becomes sexual, he thinks it is private between him and her. But she has other designs on his sexual privacy. Everything from the size of his penis, to the way he kisses is now public information and is made available to the "committee" of her friends. That is why they smirk when they finally meet him. They know, or think they know, the ins and outs of his sexuality. And he is totally unaware that the leak in intelligence is actually coming from his own girl "friend".

This loyalty deficiency does not fully bloom until the third year of marriage. It is by then that she has uncovered most of his flaws and her friends are bored with hearing about them over and over. The marriage may linger for years after this, but it is doomed. Now her weekly, or daily, ritual consists of bitching to her friends about the inadequacies of her husband. Her friends will return with their own stories of their worthless husbands. This may continue for a few more years. The only male equivalent to this abhorrent behavior is the adolescent claim of young boys that they had sex with the school slut. Even male teenagers do not talk about their girlfriend's sexuality to other men. They feel loyal to keeping her private life between the two of them. The female of the species feels no such loyalty. Throughout their teen years, into their adult years, women talk about men and their sexual needs on a daily basis. This behavior occurs in good marriages, and ferments into vicious fodder in bad marriages. If the marriage degrades to the point that divorce is the only option, women then show their true selves. The male usually does not involve the children. But that does not hold true for the female.   She is the first to file for divorce. She is the first to try and justify her actions even to the youngest of children. She will not care that the child does not understand what she is saying. The child is only feeling the pain of losing his, or her family. The female of the species becomes a 'Handmaiden of Satan' when it comes time for divorce. She has pulled the last piece of dignity from her husband, and now it is time for the death blow to his nobility as the children's father. The loyalty to family and the values that have been instilled in the children become hazy shades of gray when the female begins her final trampling of her husband's dreams. She will hold no punches, no task, or word, from wrenching his life to shreds. There is no loyalty to her husband, or to her children. The children must stand by as their mother destroys their father's standing in their eyes. They will be told of how he did not meet her needs. His sex life is now public knowledge, as twisted by the soon-to-be ex-wife. Everywhere he goes he is seen through eyes that view him in poor regard. There is no loyalty to family as the Handmaiden of Satan spews forth her venomous rage regardless of the damage that it is doing to her family. Then she has a vision. It is the vision of the female, living with the new male, while her husband, writhing in emotional agony, pays for it all.

Ω

Maternal instincts are a myth. The family is held together by the husband.

From the 1890's to the present, women have been whining for equal rights. Their battle cry is that they have been oppressed. They have been enslaved by a dominant male population. They have not been allowed to flourish and become who they wanted to be because of the oppressive tactics of the male dominated society. They were herded into sweatshops and made to work 16-hour days. Conscripted into military service, against their will, shipped off to foreign lands and told to kill people they had never even met before. They were trucked deep into mines and forced to mine coal and die of black lung disease. Required to pay for their spouses' lawyer while their other half destroyed their family and had blatant affairs with members of the opposite sex, humiliating and embarrassing them in front of their children and family...oh, wait a minute, that didn't happen to women- it happened to men. Could it be that the real sex that needed to be liberated was the male of the species?

What did women need to be liberated from? They are biologically suited to raising children. So, for the last few thousand years of human evolution, that is exactly what they have been doing. They have not been oppressed. They have not been held back. As a matter of fact up until the 1960's the housewife was held in high esteem. Their position was highly regarded by all aspects of society. But then the basic unhappiness of women, coupled with a confused society, became the basis of the greatest biological crime of the history of the species. Women were liberated from heaven and told to live in the real world. It was not the women that was being oppressed; it was the man. And he is still enslaved in an unfair culture as of the printing of this book. The last one hundred years stands as solid testament to the cultural, financial, and emotional chaining of the human male.

It is the male that holds the family together, despite years of oppression and subjugation. He's a strong beast of burden. The male of the species has been forced to endure tyranny of his being since the beginning of recorded history. Beginning at the dawn of the Industrial Revolution the male has proven that he will endure any hardship that ambles down his road to land on his back and hold on with sharpened claws. Around the turn of the century men were farmers. They dug the earth with iron tools, chopped down trees with axes, and nurtured crops that should not have grown. They spent the entire day out in the hot sun, endured blistering summers, froze the tips of their fingers off in the winter, fought off varmints in the middle of the night, and still spent time with their wives and children. During the industrial revolution many farmers could not make ends meet so they joined the throngs of other beaten men to work long hours in factories. Smoke and chemical filled they swept the floors, pumped the foot presses, stoked the steel mill furnaces while their skin was burned off. Other men drove trucks for hundreds of miles each day on bumpy, muddy roads. Their wives, in the meantime, slept at home and played with the children. Men left their home before the sun came up and returned long after it went down. They worked on assembly lines, putting the same part on a machine they could not afford daily for their entire lives. They lost fingers in industrial accidents, maimed in substandard farm equipment, burned in mill fires. They were beaten for striking for better working conditions, and they were beaten when they did not strike for better working conditions. I remember my own father's hands, worn down, calloused, grey vestiges at the tips lacking any resemblance of what was once a fingernail. His hands were always greasy, his eyes tired, his body broken and canted in the direction of the least painful stance by age forty. Yet still he managed to muster the energy to throw me a few baseballs so I could get some hitting practice in before the big little league game of the week. My grandfather had lost his hearing working in a factory that was so loud you could not hear the whistle that signaled break time unless you were standing right next to it (which, by itself, could blow out your ears!). Each day for thirty years the banging of massive solid iron machinery would slam his eardrum farther into his ear canal shredding the tissue attachment piece by piece and dulling his aural perception. By the time he was fifty he could barely hear his children as they played in the yard. The tissue eventually gave out, worn out from extreme use and abuse. Earplugs were not used in his day. His knees were shot from standing in one place for twenty five years. He walked with a sideways gait, favoring one knee, kind of like a big penguin. As kids we laughed at him and made fun when he wasn't around. He developed ulcers from worrying about being laid off from the miserable plant if the economy changed. He smoked to stave off the boredom of rote manual labor, the cigarettes taking his wind and blackening his lungs. He drank beer when he could afford it. And he came home happy to see his kids only to be demoralized by his unliberated wife's incessant nagging. No matter how hard he worked it wasn't enough. Not enough money, not enough yard work, not enough painting, not enough sex, not enough time with the kids. When he died he was old beyond his years, a man whose dreams had been smothered out of his life on a grueling daily basis. A man that could not give up because he had nowhere else to go to support his wife and children. He was representative of men of the last one hundred years. Maybe even the last thousand. Oppressed. Repressed. Put down, shut down, and let down. The veterans of wars that they did not start, and maybe didn't believe in, but went to fight anyway. Returning home with their arms, legs, and faces blown off. Men burnt beyond recognition only to be denied anything but the most difficult job in a raunchy mill town. And the persecution of men did not stop at racial lines. Blacks were routinely denied all but the lowest paying jobs. Blacks were whipped, beaten, humiliated and lynched without so much as a trial. Not black women, black men. Oppression? Men have cornered the market on oppression, repression, and depression since the inception of organized society. And men have been oppressed ten- fold more during the Industrial Revolution than women could even imagine. While women lived lives of privilege and power. Who decided the sexual events for the night? The hardworking man? Anyone who has been married for more than a year knows the answer to that question. What was the reward of a man that worked his fingers to the bone all week? Why he got to mow the lawn, fix the fence, repair the shed and till the garden. He didn't get to pick the fruits and vegetables from the garden; that was the domain of his ex-wife. He got to go to bed with unfulfilled sexual desires, and dream dreams that would never come true. Die slowly as the chemicals of his workplace sliced through the cells of his body like shards of miniature glass. Men are the ones that need to be liberated. It is the male in society that is the slave, not women. It is men that need emancipation, not women. A slave has no freedom; monitored from dusk to dawn and then held captive until the sun rises. In a marriage one person fits that role- the husband. He is forced to go to work each day to provide for the family. Throughout history the women have stayed home, unsupervised with the freedom to do as they pleased. There was always housework but that could usually be done in a short time, or even minimized by nagging the husband to pick up after himself or force the kids to clean their areas better. There was no oppression here. Sitting home, drinking coffee, smoking cigarettes, talking to the other wives about their husbands. Meanwhile the man of the house was out taking orders from his boss at a job he couldn't stand.

Think that this treatment is unique to our era? Consider the nursery rhyme, the Farmer in the Dell.

> The farmer in the dell
> The farmer in the dell
> Hi-ho, the derry-o
> The farmer in the dell
> The farmer takes a wife
> The farmer takes a wife
> Hi-ho, the derry-o
> The farmer takes a wife
> The wife takes a child
> The wife takes a child
> Hi-ho, the derry-o
> The wife takes a child

Well, you know the rest. They guy is inundated with rats, cats, children, and a piece of cheese that he can't even eat. He should have stayed single and he knows it. But he, like millions of other men, endured because it was the right thing to do for their family.

5

THE PURSUIT OF MEN

Appetizer
Gordon's London Dry Gin

Main Course
Foster's Lager

Most women need to get a life that does not revolve around men. When you watch women in groups, or listen to their conversations, they are usually discussing men. Throughout history, women have been socially conditioned to become an object of desire for men. This brainwashing begins in early childhood. Women have never had to develop past this position because it has been a successful strategy for survival. This evolutionary holding pattern accounts for the difficulty that men have when attempting to speak intellectually with women. Today's media reinforces the position of women as "sex objects" while promoting men as "success objects".

Observation of the lack of intellectual development can be observed in young females. It is seen in female toddlers in their manner of play. The toys that children play with reflect their future behavior. In other words, children play in the method in which they will act as adults. We see this in the animal world. Young wolves wrestle and fight to show who the dominant wolf will be. Fledgling birds flap their wings. Fish, while in the egg, vigorously beat their tail. Young human beings play with toys. Toys of their choosing. The toys have become more elaborate as the technology advances. Boys play Nintendo, shooting down the bad guys in war simulation games, scoring touchdowns in football games, and racing around the track in car simulation games. All indicators of future adult behavior for boys. Girls play with dolls. Barbie dolls dominated the scene for years. And then came the women's movement. The great equalizer. Years of male oppression was now ended. The human female was going to be an equal to the human male. Fair was fair. Our biological evolution was going to be matched by our social evolution. Men and women were going to do the same jobs, tasks, sports and activities - exactly the same. Men agreed to this new style of living with tongue in cheek. Sure, men said, women can do everything that men can do, we won't try to stop you anymore. As usual, men agreed with women; your station in life is all our fault. The revolution had begun. And the first step was to change the way young girls were "socialized."

Everything was going to be different in the future world of even-handedness. Except for one small thing. It never happened. Young girls did not rush out and buy GI Joe dolls and set up small skirmishes with their brothers. The Daisy Manufacturing Company did make little pink BB guns - but they sat on the store shelves because girls were simply not interested in BB guns. All the Women's Liberation rhetoric in the world could not change that. The majority of young girls did not join the hockey team and knock pucks (and heads), around the ice. Yes, there were a few noteworthy cases were mothers pushed their daughters to compete with boys, but they were the odd case. The minority in extremis. It's not surprising that these odd cases made the evening news because they were atypical. The young lass playing on the football team. The ambitious girl on the boys' baseball team. These cases were media events, not the future course of behavior for the human species. So socialization was not the answer.

Society was not brainwashing their young boys and girls to play with different toys. Boys and girls just preferred to play with different toys. Along the way the female humans became confused as to what their role was supposed to be. Experiments with our closest genetic relatives substantiates this claim.

According to Gerianne Alexander, professor of Psychology at Texas A& M University, male and female monkeys show preferences for certain toys. The hypothesis was fairly simple: What would a monkey choose if given a choice of many different toys? The results paralleled the human studies. Alexander's conclusions showed that, when given a choice of a selection of toys, the male monkeys spent a majority of their time playing with trucks, cars, and balls. The female monkeys spent a majority of their time playing with dolls and other classically female toys. Alexander concluded that females monkeys prefer dolls because nature selected for them to care for newborns. The male monkeys showed preferences for toys that involve three dimensional space such as moving and throwing. Alexander summarizes with the statement, "Sex-related object preference appeared early in human evolution.", according to Alexander, "Masculine toys and feminine toys," Alexander says, "are clearly categories constructed by people. However, our finding that male and female vervet monkeys show similar preferences for these toys as boys and girls do, suggests that what makes a 'boy toy' and a 'girl toy' is more than just what society dictates. It suggests that there may be perceptual cues that attract males or females to particular objects such as toys.". So much for the "Everybody's the Same" movement. That is unless there is a worldwide conspiracy that has infiltrated deeply into the simian world. Could this be true? Consider the following Evening News Anchor reporting this anomaly.

INTERIOR. CAMERA SHOT OF BOTH ANCHOR AND SIDEKICK SITTING AT THE NEWS DESK, STRAIGHTENING PAPERS AND PREPARING TO FACE THE CAMERA.

Jane Smiley, Evening News Anchor: "And finally tonight, we have a story of worldwide conspiracy that begins with two monkeys that were arrested in a little town south of Dallas, Texas.

Jim Dandy, Evening News sidekick: "Monkeys?"

Jane Smiley, Evening News Anchor: "Yes, monkeys."

Jim Dandy, Evening News sidekick: "Well, please, go right ahead. The suspense is too much."

INTERIOR. TIGHT CAMERA SHOT OF ANCHOR CLOSEUP ON HIS FACE AND SHOULDERS.

Jane Smiley, Evening News Anchor: "Tonight we have a story that goes beyond the bounds of primate decency. We begin with a report from our field reporter."

EXTERIOR. FIELD REPORTER OUTSIDE SEEDY WAREHOUSE IN A RUNDOWN INDUSTRIAL AREA.

Field Reporter: "Thanks, Jim. I am standing here outside a warehouse where earlier today two velvet, uh, vervet monkeys were arrested in an alleged scam that was designed to mislead liberals into thinking all boys and girls think the same."

Jane Smiley, Evening News Anchor: "Have you found any information as to what was happening? What type of a 'scam' was it?"

Field Reporter: "Well, it appears that these monkeys were involved with a few of the major toy manufacturers in a conspiracy to limit the beliefs of humans. The monkeys were part of a study that showed young male and young female monkeys chose certain toys according to their sex. My source tells me that the young males agreed to choose toys like cars and trucks; while the young females chose dolls."

Jane Smiley, Evening News Anchor: "Uh, did you find any evidence that showed, uh, why the monkeys stooped to such a low level?"

Field Reporter: "Well, that's because of the iliac crest. It is higher in monkeys, therefore they cannot stand up straight. Plus the muscle from the hip is shorter, so that's what makes them......"

Jane Smiley, Evening News Anchor: "No, no, no. I know why monkeys cannot walk upright. Let me reword this. Why did they get involved with such a low-life scheme?"

Field Reporter: "Oh, the scheme. Yeah, yeah, apparently the monkeys wanted the money to buy bananas. Once again, it's about the money. I also heard that some of the monkeys were influenced by some liberal college professors. I heard a report that one monkey even had relatives at the Xerxes Primate Institute and was notified his family would get preferential treatment. Also, one monkey was promised that he would be a test pilot on the next Shuttle mission. Poor guys didn't realize that NASA stopped that program over 50 years ago. I will continue to investigate and report back to you as the situation develops. Back to you, Jane."

Jane Smiley, Evening News Anchor: "Yes, monkeys gone bad. This is Jane Smiley signing off."

Sounds ludicrous doesn't it? As ludicrous as the idea that men and women are the same. Two monkeys arrested in an alleged conspiracy so vast it would make a Drinking Man shudder. So let's be more scientific and realistic. There is no conspiracy. The most logical explanation is that young primates have developed preferences for certain toys based on the innate sexual differences of their brain. Boys will be boys, girls will be girls. Since monkeys are not influenced by societal pressures like humans, this study suggests that the differences between male and female behavior could be instinctual based on biological differences inherent in each sexes brain. Did the female and male brain evolve different ways to respond to the environment? The idea that male and female brains are structured differently has been at the forefront of many intellectual investigations. Remember that most brain research has shown that there are clear differences in the way that men and women process emotions, language, comprehension, and general information(such as directions!).

Toy sales did not change because young girls did not want GI Joe. They wanted Barbie, and Barbie's unrelated future progeny – Bratz dolls, MyScene dolls and accessories, Cabbage Patch Kids, Polly Pocket, and the various other dolls that inundate the market each year. Dolls that cry, puke and piss themselves continue to sell in record amounts to young girls. And each one has her own way to attract a mate and set up a house to live happily ever after in. All accessories were aligned to men, marriage, and babies. They sold like hotcakes. This left Mattel, manufacturers of Barbie, wondering how to change Barbie into a more marketable commodity. Being good businessmen, they did not listen to the rhetoric of the Women's Liberation movement. They listened to their market. As a result, Barbie did change. She became more feminine, and more diversified in her femininity. The Barbie dolls that sold were not "Barbie the lawyer" or "Barbie the doctor" but Barbie the rock star and Barbie the model. But Barbie the young, eligible single girl fashionably dressing to attract a mate broke all sales records. Young girls did not, and still do not, want to be boys; biology has selected them for reproductive purposes, simply put - to be girls. The "equality" that a few hardened women (with daddy problems) had fought for was evidenced in the sale of toys to innocent young girls. Like rock star Cyndi Lauper said, "Girls Just Wanna Have Fun", and fun for little girls is playing house with dolls and other symbols of their future roles. There is nothing wrong with that. Females play with dolls, set up house, and obsess with their appearance at a young age. This behavior carries on into adult life when they will spend their days fixated on men. And after they "get" a man they preoccupy themselves with the man's behavior; looking to exploit their man's negative traits into a means to control the unfortunate being. And, sooner or later, the man is not exciting enough for them. The song "What Have You Done For Me Lately" comes to mind. Because any creature that is scrutinized in depth, and as often, as women scrutinize their men, is bound to have all of its flaws and weaknesses uncovered. That is why women need to get a life that does not center around the man in her life, like Barbie so intently focuses on Ken. Drink that Foster Lager.

Even the video and board games are centered around young girls' future behavior. "Mall Madness" is a board game for girls that gives the player a certain amount of money and they go on a virtual shopping tour. This seems to step outside the boundaries of entrenched female behavior. Or does it? A female going to the mall to spend money she hasn't earned? Gee, that sounds like real life. Find a girl under ten that has not heard of the video game "Mall Madness". Most of the video games are targeted to boys. The only ones that girls enjoy are games that mimic their future role as an wife and mother. "DigiMakeover" is a popular video game with girls. In this cerebral challenge the young girls pick out different clothes that they are going to wear with different accessories and makeup. No rocket science here, just coordinating the right socks with the right handbag. This game does not include solving global issues, or ways to work out the world population problem. It does not talk about new inventions, or space flight. It deals with how to dress properly so that you are fashionable while attracting a mate. But it does not end with the toys that females choose; it actually begins there. It can be proven over and over each time you hear two females in conversation.

There is an old adage: small minds talk about people, mediocre minds talk about events, and great minds talk about ideas. A majority of their inter-female dialogue is about men. If you listen in on these banterings, the topic is usually not how wonderful the men in their life are. When was the last time a group of women sat around to discuss a trip to Mars? Or ways to prevent global warming? These conversations may fleetingly take place but usually end up as a man-bashing session. When women groups meet they are usually to discuss relationships, or how they were mis-used by men, or how they can cope with the horrible habits of men. There are even some women's groups that meet under the guise of living a life without men. Guess what the topic of discussion usually turns to? Yes sirree, Bob. Men. Here is the transcript of one of those meetings, secretly ob-tained at great danger to a colleague of mine. Take a sip before you read.

"Okay ladies, let's quiet down. I would like to begin our meeting tonight. First let us welcome our newcomers to the "Life without Men Association."(round of applause) Well, let's begin. Amy, we left off on you, Amy, last week. Would you like to share your feeling with the group?"

"Hi, my name is Amy."

"HI, AMY!", explodes in unison, reminiscent of an AA meeting.

"Hi…uh, I am just getting over a relationship with Brian. I thought he was everything I ever needed until… sob…sob…until I found out he was married. (sob, sob, sob…sob, sob, sob, sob).

"The bastard!", replies the group leader.

"They're all the same.", chimes in her 38-year-old-twenty-pounds-overweight-never-been-married-manhating-daddy-never-loved-me-sidekick.

"Anyway, that is the last straw, I have decided to live my life without being hurt by some man. (cheers, applause)

"That's right! Starting tonight, I am a liberated woman. No more men. Before Brian, it was Keith - a stockbroker. We dated for almost two years. One day I found two plane tickets to the Bahamas in his jacket. When I accidentally looked at them, I found that they were for him and his secretary. He was such a jerk. He said I was too sexually repressed and judgmental. He could have told me. I would have been better off if he just told me. I would have understood. I met Keith through a friend just after college, when Wayne and I broke up...."

The conversation continued for three hours that night. (The entire transcript is available upon request.) Each female got a turn to whine and complain about how they were put upon and abused by men. They bonded like primitive berry pickers that night. But notoriously absent from the discussion was what they were going to do with their lives. There was no discussion of starting a business that was going to revolutionize the computer industry. There was no discussion of organizing a group to feed the homeless. There was no discussion to help support their local political candidate in his bid for office. There was only discussion about men. All night long the topic was men. And how horrible men were. In order to truly liberate themselves, women need to get a life that does not center around men.

Ω

Television programming for women keeps women at a evolutionary standstill. Women's television does not show women how to improve their lives. They just reinforce the emptiness that women feel from watching rehashed stereotypes of how to try to get a man to make them happy. Television shows such as "Desperate Housewives" depict how inept and insensitive men are in relationships. But what do the desperate housewives do to overcome these insensitive and inept men? They have affairs with other men! And before each episode is over, the desperate housewives are complaining about their new men as being inept and insensitive! Go figure. These women give off the message to other women that the way to overcome your wretched lives, your hopeless relationship with your husband, is to have another unfulfilled relationship with another man. There are no television shows that are designed for women to evolve socially. Where are the television shows that give women a boost that are trying to better themselves by achieving something? Some home improvement shows are coming close, but the majority of the work, and ideas, are being completed by men, gay men, but men nonetheless. The History Channel is targeted primarily to men. National Geographic, Discovery, the Learning Channel - all watched primarily by the male of the species. Most learning channels are targeted towards men. Why don't women want to learn? Why don't they want to get a better life? Is it easier just to blame men? When given the choice of taking a chance and becoming a better human being most women fall short. This conditioning starts at a young age. The majority of movies that are targeted towards females portray the girl as the pursued and the man as the pursuer.

You can hardly think of a Disney movie that does not have the young girl pursued by the young man. In Snow White she is surrounded by seven men, all not worthy of her sexual charms. She lies in wait until she is rendered helpless by the wicked Queen. The wicked Queen wants to be the "fairest of them all" and is told by her mirror that she is not. The deep psychological overtones here are amazing. Most women spend hours in front of their mirror; especially the "pretty" ones. When another girl is found to be "prettier" than her they verbally berate her(behind her back, of course). In Snow White the Queen asks her mirror every day. Now the queen was the most beautiful woman in all the land, and very proud of her beauty. She had a mirror, which she stood in front of every morning, and asked:

      "Mirror, mirror, on the wall,
      Who in this land is fairest of all?"

And the mirror always said:

      "You, my queen, are fairest of all."

And then she knew for certain that no one in the world was more beautiful than she.

    Now Snow-White grew up, and when she was seven years old, she was so beautiful, that she surpassed even the queen herself. Now when the queen asked her mirror:

      "Mirror, mirror, on the wall,
      Who in this land is fairest of all?"

The mirror said:

      "You, my queen, are fair; it is true.
      But Little Snow-White is still
      A thousand times fairer than you."

When the queen heard the mirror say this, she became pale with envy, and from that hour on, she hated Snow-White. Whenever she looked at her, she thought that Snow-White was to blame that she was no longer the most beautiful woman in the world. This turned her heart around. Her jealousy gave her no peace. Finally she summoned a huntsman and said to him,

      "Take Snow-White out into the woods to a
      remote spot, and stab her to death. As proof
      that she is dead bring her lungs and her liver
      back to me. I shall cook them with salt and eat
      them."

    Lest I remind you that this is a fairy tale from the Grimm Brothers, Jacob and Wilhelm. The Grimm brothers made a name for themselves by collecting, and rewriting, the stories that had been passed from village to village for centuries. The tale of Snow White has been in the collective psyche of females for centuries. It is the brutality of the story that stands out.

"Take Snow-White out into the woods to a remote spot, and stab her to death. As proof that she is dead bring her lungs and her liver back to me. I shall cook them with salt and eat them."

This is what we are teaching our young girls. No wonder they are so confused by the time they get to high school. We are teaching them that their only worth is to be pursued by men. The more men that pursue them- the greater their significance. Consider the other Disney movies. In Cinderella she is nothing until her beauty attracts a man that searches the world for her. Once he finds her they live happily ever after.

In The Little Mermaid we are told that women are nothing without their prince.

In Sleeping Beauty we are told that until the women is kissed by her man, she will remain in a euphemistic coma.

Beauty and the Beast. Even though he is ugly, she agrees to fall in love for him.

Aladdin. Pocahontas. The list goes on and on...

Even the Playboy Channel, that bastion of liberal female sexual expression, is not exempt from female obsession with males lives. Playboy has a show called "Foursome", a weekly series that outlines the interactions between two couples that have just met and are given a limo, a beautiful house, and every reason to have sex. The cameras follow the couples around for three days. After meeting on one episode the males and females pair off and go to different rooms to discuss the evenings' events. The two men shake hands and talk about everything that they are doing with their lives. The conversation bounces around from hang gliding to football to their work. The men briefly mention the two women in the other room. The camera then swings over to the girls' room. The discussion centers totally around the men; their physical attributes, their personality, hair color, eyes, demeanor, and every other aspect of their being is brought forth for scrutiny. It appears that even in the highly sexually-charged atmosphere of Playboy women have nothing else going on in their minds except men. The Drinking Man realizes that women are piggybacking onto the lives of men. If women are to truly be the equal to men they need to evolve socially. Social evolution is based upon improving the method of their interactions with other human beings. The human female communication system still revolves around the subject that they have thrashed around for centuries – men. This skirts the theory of evolution and brings us to a different idea- one of Social Darwinism.

Ω

Social Darwinism is survival of the fittest in communal animals. Man is a communal animal. In nature, the strongest beast out competes all the others to pass on his genes to the next generation. Subtle mutations and genetic variance is either selected for –or against. The same may be happening in pack animals. The individual with the most adept social skills will reap the most benefits from the pack. One of the most advantageous social skills is effective communication. If a wolf is able to read the body language of another wolf, he will know when the wolf is angry, tired, happy, sad, or feeling sick. Wolves have an intricate social structure. The pack is ruled by an Alpha male. It is always a male, never a female. This Alpha male is the most stressed in the pack because everyone wants his job. There is a distinct "pecking order" among the wolves that are below the alpha male. This pecking order is established by a series of growls, barks, grunts, and a myriad of body postures. The height of the tail sends a variety of signals among males. The term "tail between his legs" has a direct meaning in the wolf world. It is very advantageous to survival that you understand the messages that are being sent in the strict social order of a wolf. But this communication system exists mainly amongst male wolves. The females have a rudimentary communication system as outlined in the first chapter. It is the male wolf that is able to read the other wolves intentions, size up the other wolves abilities compared to his own abilities, and make a decision as to fight or flee, that is the most successful in the pack. He lives to pass on his genes to other wolves. This is an example of Social Darwinism, survival of the most communicative. It is here where human females can take charge of their own plight. Women must see that they exist in society subservient to men by their own doing. If they want to move up the evolutionary social scale they must evolve in their own way separate from men (but in the same direction). But they seem to lack a direction in which to travel.

The organism that is able to read more than one mode of communication to understand the intent of its fellow organisms would have an advantage over those with lesser skills. This organism, be it a wolf, a musk ox, or a human being, would be able to read what each of its pack members are feeling. These feelings would be interpreted by the skillful one and used to help it in its own survival. The theory of Social Darwinism promotes the higher ranking individuals because of their status, achievement and the facility to collaborate in the pack. The higher ranking individuals in a society will have more offspring and solidify their position. Okay, now apply the theory of Social Darwinism to women. This will help explain why women lag behind socially. In today's society they do not need to be great communicators, great inventors, great thinkers, or great athletically-they just have to be great at obtaining the attentions of a great man. Socially, women compete against other women for men. Once she gets a man, she has to entice the man to stick around. The women that did that best was awarded by the pack with a place to live, some status, and security for her children. Social Darwinism precluded natural selection for intelligence and inventiveness in women. As long as women are happy with living through their men-they will continue to stay where they are evolutionarily.

This lack of direction appears to have a biological foundation. Biology dictates that the female play no other role in society than to reproduce and raise children. This being the case, we cannot fault women for their lack of independent goals. It would be just as unfair to blame a frog for bumping his ass every time he jumped. It's not the frog's fault he was designed by nature for a certain task. We may not discuss it in polite circles but frogs do eat a lot of dirty little bugs that would otherwise fly around willy-nilly and drive us all crazy. So all creatures may have a purpose. But is that the state of affairs with female human beings? Are women not in possession of human brains? Are there not women that have exceeded the accomplishments of many men? Do we not have women scientists, doctors, and even astronauts? Even women politicians?

The answer is yes. These women have made a life for themselves. But these women are in the marginally accepted group (read minority). The preponderance of women in America depend upon their men for their "raison d'être." The greater part of heterosexual relationships are usually based on the cavewoman logic of "bring me something." Back in the cave days, women felt good if the man they chose was very good at bringing home the bacon. Women became addicted to a man's attention in the form of food and gifts. They would smirk at other women when they received something that the other women did not receive. This is not entirely an ego-driven desire. This contributed to the survival of the women, and the survival of her children. The smirk may have been a cavewoman's way of saying, "I am not going to starve, and neither are my children."

Take another drink.

Let's look at the behavior of some successful women to see if this theory holds water.

Valentina Tereshkova flew aboard Vostok 6 on June 16, 1963. Tereshkova was not a pilot. She was an amateur parachutist. This was the closest the Russians could find for a qualified women astronaut so they enrolled her in their space program. Tereshkova circled the Earth 48 times in 70 hours 50 minutes. She spent more time in orbit than all the U.S. Mercury astronauts combined. Valentina Tereshkova received the Order of Lenin and Hero of the Soviet Union awards from the Russian government. She served as the president of the Soviet Women's Committee and became a member of the USSR's national parliament within the Soviet. Their storybook Russian marriage (the ceremony was attended by Soviet Premier Nikita Kruschev) ended in divorce because she was not "fulfilled". She had been into space, made a national hero, and still blamed her husband for an unfulfilled life. He was not enough for her. Here is a woman that had a life, and nevertheless blamed her man for being unfulfilled. The female mindset is hard to break. Now we can say that the Soviets, under communism, just didn't pick the right people for the astronaut corps. Certainly that was an isolated incident. Well, America has its own female astronaut story.

NASA astronaut Lisa Marie Nowak was one of NASA's rising stars. She had a degree in Aeronautical Engineering from the U. S. Naval Academy, and was commissioned in May of 1985. Nowak was assigned to JSC's Shuttle Training Aircraft Branch at Ellington, Texas. She spent over ten years working, being evaluated, and groomed for the Astronaut Corps. In April 1996, Nowak was selected by NASA and spent two years of rigorous astronaut training and evaluation. Every weakness and fault is considered during this standard astronaut preparation. She became qualified for flight status as a mission specialist. Nowak was assigned technical duties in the CAPCOM Branch and worked in Mission Control as the prime communicator with the shuttle crews. She was top notch. Nowak was selected as mission specialist on STS-121 and spent thirteen days in space. Nowak was responsible for operating the remote arm during scheduled space walks. Nowak received NASA's highest marks. Nowak was married and the mother of three children.

But NASA did not take into account that Nowak was a woman.

Nowak drove one thousand miles—wearing diapers so she would not have to stop—to attack a fellow astronaut in a parking lot outside the Orlando Airport. She drove this entire distance, ruined her career, devastated her family, and for what? Was she upset that the other astronaut had bumped her for the next space shuttle flight? Did the other astronaut sabotage her career somehow? Was the other astronaut going to expose a scandal of some sort? None of the above. The other astronaut, a female named Colleen Shipman, was romantically involved with the man that Lisa Nowak was formerly involved with. Even in the Astronaut Corps, women are women first and astronauts second.

Ω

Think of famous women throughout history. Did they ever really build or invent anything? Is there any tangible evidence that they made something for future generations to enjoy? Cleopatra was the Queen of Egypt, had thousands of lovers, and that was about it. She was not known for building great cities, fighting great battles with superior military strategy, or even for enacting fair laws for her people. She was Queen because she was the daughter of the Pharoah Ptolemy VII. What was her reign of Queen marked by? She got laid a lot. Did not really do much else. As a matter of fact she was the one that squandered Egypt after thousands of years of solid rule. After her rule Egypt was conquered by Rome and became a Roman territory. Other women were famous for who they were married to. Dolly

Madison did very little to advance the struggle of mankind against a harsh planet; but she is famous because she was married to a United States President. But what did she actually do? Attend a few fundraisers? Big deal.

Not to sound condescending of female history, there were, and are, many famous singers, artists, and writers. But it is the atypical female human that makes history based solely on her accomplishments.

This is a generalization only because it is true for most women. The marginally accepted group will definitely take offense at this *broad* generalization. Women in the vein of Margaret Brown (the Unsinkable Molly Brown) should be offended that such a generalization is made that could include them. But women like Margaret Brown do not fit into the mold that characterizes so many American "common" females. Margaret Brown was not one of the common females of American society. Margaret often traveled to Europe to study drama, music, literature and languages. She was a complete human, being independent of her husband's life. Molly Brown had her own life. A life she made for herself. She was most known for being a passenger on the unfortunate luxury ship the Titanic. She became a legend for her behavior during the sinking. Once pulled from the water, she distinguished herself amongst the passengers by passing out food, drinks, and blankets aboard the rescue ship, Carpathia. Margaret Brown had made a life for herself before and after the Titanic tragedy. She was a well- rounded human being. Margaret's life broadened after the Titanic sank in 1912. She became a celebrity for her gallant efforts when news of her heroics reached New York. Margaret used this familiarity to promote her beliefs in women's rights. During World War I, Margaret went on a voyage to France to establish a relief position for the soldiers. She taught herself French so she could converse with the locals. Margaret did not see much of her husband during these years; Margaret was living her own life. From

1929 to 1932 Margaret spent her time between living in New York and traveling. She returned to Leadville occasionally to visit family and friends. On October 26, 1932, at the age of sixty-five, the "Unsinkable Molly Brown" passed away from a stroke. Margaret Brown was active in politics and in 1914 became the first woman to run for the U.S. Congress. She lost the campaign, but won a life for herself that did not depend on running some poor sap into the ground emotionally and physically. We should be raising our daughters to act more like Molly Brown and less like "Mean Girls".

There are many other women that have socially evolved. Yet, these women are usually vilified by the common female. They teach about them in school as sideshow attractions. Look at the freak. This is what women have to do that cannot permanently attach themselves to a man.

The sneer of not staying home and attaching your emotional life's umbilical to your husband pervades every mention of names like Amelia Earhart, Susan B. Anthony, Sojourner Truth, and Leona Helmsly. Yet the common female disdains those that have made a life for themselves. Why?

Men do not usually disdain other famous men that have ventured out. Men make heroes out of brave and daring men. They teach their sons to have the qualities of these men. Young boys idolize astronauts like John Glenn of Friendship 7, baseball players like Tony Conigliaro of the Boston Red Sox, and pirates like Long John Silver. Young boys play act that they are these heroes. Cowboys and Indians. Cops and Robbers. Pirates. Diving on the bed and catching the winning touchdown in the Super Bowl. Just like their hero. Hitting the home run that wins the world series. Just like their hero.

Where are the female heroes?

When you watch young girls play dolls you see what is in store for their husbands. "Someone" is usually ostracized in these activities. "Someone" is usually married to the rich guy. And all of the dolls usually go shopping. Each doll is dressed in the latest fashion. Dolls set the stage for the way females treat men in later life. We can change this. Someday. If only we could get young girls to engage in fulfilling leisure time activities.

Most mental health professionals agree that physical activity is a safeguard against depression. Sitting around all day mulling over the same problems is what leads most women to these destructive behaviors. It's common knowledge that physical inactivity is associated with increased risk for heart disease, diabetes, and osteoporosis . Yet the amount of women that actively undergo physical activity is declining. Despite the benefits of physical activity, less than half of the women in the United States engage in any leisure-time physical activity.

Dr. James Kruger, PhD, Division of Nutrition and Physical Activity, of the Center for Disease Control collected data from the Behavioral Risk Factor Surveillance System for the year 2004. The data was collected on men and women 18 years of age and older. The survey sample was 296,971 in 2004 for 50 states and the District of Columbia . The results showed that men are increasing their physical activity. Aware of the effects of inactivity on brain function and body metabolism, men are increasing their intellectual and biological capabilities. Women, according to the study, are less active than men. In 2004, the Center for Disease control study showed that over 26% of women had absolutely no physical leisure time activity. That is one out of every four women. These women do absolutely no exercising at all. No wonder day time television talk shows have such a large audience. Instead of working, or at least working out, one out of every four women are completely sedentary, doing nothing to keep fit whatsoever. Not even a brisk walk once a week. No wonder they have nothing better to do than wait to unload their unhappiness on some unsuspecting man. Women also do not participate in hobbies as frequently as men.

Of the hundreds of different hobbies that Americans participate in- less than a dozen are dominated by women. Amateur radio, photography, model railroad building, and woodworking are traditionally male dominated hobbies. Surprisingly so is gardening, cooking, and bird watching. These three hobbies are stereotypically characterized as enjoyed by females, but statistics prove otherwise. Coin and stamp collecting are the hobbies of men that sometimes are started when they are children. Young girls do not have similar interests. Females do not participate in hobbies to this extent. Or to any extent, for that matter. Women get into hobbies when they get older (and there are no more men left to nag). The only hobbies that are dominated by a great quantity of females are crocheting, embroidery, and quilting. Yet these pastimes do not have near the numbers that the top male hobbies have. It appears that women do not actively participate in hobbies, although they could benefit from them. Girls of high school age engage in scrap booking. This very self-centered activity revolves around the young girl and her possessions.

According to Howard Tinsley, Professor emeritus of Psychology at Southern Illinois University, hobbies contribute to your physical and mental health. Having a hobby also helps people become healthier, happier and have a higher regard for overall life satisfaction. In his book, Psychological Benefits of Leisure Participation, Tinsley summarizes 15 years of research that involved more than 4,000 people. Tinsley found that people with hobbies had more fulfilled lives. Consider the following exchange between sisters that have husbands with similar interests.

"Where is your husband?"

"He's down in the cellar working on his silly trains."

"Trains? Oh, Gawd! He's just as bad as my Charley."

"I did not know that Charley was into train sets. How long has he been doing that?"

"Too long! He started when my oldest moved out of the house. Built a silly little mountain, or hill, whatever it was, in the boy's bedroom on a piece of plywood."

"At least he hasn't taken over the whole cellar! I can hardly walk down there. John has turned the entire thing into a miniature city. He's down there day and night. Hardly even talks to me anymore. I wish he spent half the time fiddling with my gadgets as he does with those silly lights and switches."

(Both ladies laugh.)

"I mean it's crazy. He's like a little kid playing with a train set."

"Mine, too. What do they say? The only difference between men and boys is the size of their toys."

"Don't get me started on the size of his 'toy'!"

(Raucous laughter.)

"I'm serious. Just the money he spends. I saw a receipt for one train that cost $28.00. I mean we're not hurting for money…but twenty eight dollars? I just think it is ludicrous to spend twenty eight bucks on a little train."

"That's how Charlie is. He spent over a hundred dollars last month on streetlights for his set. He's down there day and night trying to keep them lit. They never work right. Cussing and swearing every time one goes out. Like he is King of the Lilliputians. Shoot, I ask him to change the light over the stove and it takes a week."

(Cooperative laughter.)

"I guess it isn't as bad as Grace's husband. He's into ham radio. She called me last week. We talked for hours. She told me he goes down there and just talks to anyone that will listen. She says he has all of these stupid radio terms that they use to go back and forth. She can't understand why they just don't speak regular English."

"Ham radio? That sounds boring. Is that the one with the big antenna in the backyard. They might as well put up a sign that says, 'Hi, my husband is so boring he talks to people about nothing all day'."

(Polite laughter.)

"Men. They have nothing better to do than to play with their little toys. Anyway, what did you and Grace talk about??

"Oh, the usual, what's happening on the soaps, our husbands, the kids; she caught me up on the latest gossip. Did you know her sister is having an affair with a guy twenty years younger than she is?"

"Get out of here! Twenty years younger? No way!"

"Yeah, that's what she said. Anyway she wants to come over tomorrow. What do you want to do?"

" Oh, I don't know. What do you want to do?"

"Gee, I don't know. Maybe we could have Charley and John cook up some ribs. Then we could have a barbecue."

"Sounds good to me. Did you hear that about Debbie? I heard from Evelyn that Vivian's husband knows a guy that saw Debbie and ..."

And the rest of the conversation slid down similarly pointless roads. No meaning, no intellect, no interest beside what everyone else was doing. Boring. If it isn't drama... Let me stop, you know the rest. Woman really need to get a life. Have you ever heard two women get excited about participating in a hobby with their husband? How many guys that are into Civil War reenactments can say their ex-wife introduced them to the hobby and encourages them to attend events? How many wives have introduced their husband to any hobby at all? Men are constantly attempting to involve their wife in something that has a little intellectual interest attached to it. From stargazing to sailing, men strive to solicit their wives to embrace a hobby, any hobby. But, alas, it is usually futile. Having a hobby that is enjoyable helps men to deal with their lot as husbands of women that have nothing better to do than to put the man under their microscope and scrutinize his every shortcoming. Hey, maybe that is their hobby- attacking their husbands! Drink up, but don't make drinking your hobby!

Ω

Even in the workplace women spend their time talking about men. According to a survey by the Office Management Association, the number one problem reported by large office managers is woman gossiping. Woman spend more time emailing, talking on the phone, and interacting with other woman, about one subject: men. Does this also apply to attractive, popular women? Even more so. Women that are attractive usually begin to feel the attentions of males from a young age. They stop getting their praise from doing a good job in school. This praise was great in elementary school. The young girl would be praised as to how smart she was just for sitting still and listening to the boring lesson that the female teacher was giving. She was commended for sitting still. The young boys in the class were habitually berated for getting out of their seat. Boys in school are routinely marked down on their grades for their behavior. School is kind to young girls. But that was not enough for the good-looking girls. They found that they could get the same praise and attention by just being alive. No work needed there. And the attention rolled in. All dependent on how good she looks. Young girls enjoy this praise for doing nothing. They begin to build their lives around it.

It is time for women to evolve from the cave days. Their happiness and survival no longer depends on what "their man" can do for them. Their happiness and survival depend on what they can do for themselves. If a woman has an empty, meaningless life she should realize that she is the cause of that, not her husband. Their husband is not the reason that they do not feel good about themselves. Anymore than their father was when they were teenagers. If women are to socially evolve to the level of men, they need to take responsibility for their happiness. They need to get a life that does not depend on taking their feelings of emptiness out on their unsuspecting husband.

6

FASHION

Appetizer
DeKuyper Apple Schnapps

Main Course
Blue Moon Full Moon

Most women are easily led when it comes to fashion. The billions of dollars that the fashion industry hauls in every year stands as testament to that. Women will buy, and wear, whatever clothes they think the other women are wearing. Women will act, and say, whatever they think other women are saying and doing. Women dance the way they see other women dancing. They light their cigarettes, drink their drinks, and brush their hair in exactly the same manner that other women do these activities. Imitation has been the advancement of women's behavior over the centuries. Women dress for other women. They want other women to look at them, not their men. In a nutshell, women behave like sheep in a flock.

Fashion has evolved in the same manner that other social ideas evolve. These ideas start out as functional and complicate themselves from there. Fashion began in the cave days. Most people think that human beings wore animal skins to keep warm. A quick look in the science book will show that most fledgling human societies lived in tropical regions. No clothes were needed to keep warm. Fashion was most likely started by fat woman to cover their bodies (The same women are suspected to have invented alcohol). These covered mammoths could hide their fat rolls. Except in the summer time. Therefore they moved north, and their men followed. Now they could keep their bodies covered for most of the year. Henceforth, the industry of fashion was born. Drink up. Here's to fashion.

Fashion is a mode of expression. It is a mode of expressing the social class that a woman is in, or wants everyone to think she is in. I recall a friend of mine that dated a young lady. If you met her, you would think that she was very wealthy. She wore Gucci, shopped at Macy's, and would reveal (without anyone asking) that she had never been inside a Wal-Mart. My friend spent hundreds of dollars on presents for her as she would not accept anything that did not have a designer label. She would actually push the present away (causing some very awkward moments).

I knew her for months before I saw her at one of the local law firms in town. She would tell everyone that she worked for ABC Law Firm. Before they could ask what she did there, she would go on about the latest case the firm was working on. She would always put herself in the middle of the case. Assuming she was an attorney, I finally asked my friend what type of law she practiced. He was dismayed and embarrassed at my ignorance. She was not a lawyer, she was the receptionist. Making about $22,000 a year. Answered the phones and took messages. She was not wealthy, nor even well off. Her father was a schoolteacher, her mother worked as a secretary for the City Parks and Recreation Department. She was a receptionist that spent every dime she made to create a facade of wealth. And that facade was not to impress men, but to impress women. Whenever I was around her she would always play "The Price is Right" about her clothes and accessories, more so if the was another female in the area. Each item of clothing would be priced by her, or asked to be priced by the nearest victim.

I remember one time in particular. We were standing just in the entrance to the mall waiting for her boyfriend to arrive. I named her Phoneymoney after James Bond's "glamour wannabe" secretary, Moneypenny. Moneypenny wanted James Bond, who just oozed wealth and class, but kept her desires somewhat hidden. Phoneymoney wanted everyone to think she had wealth and class, and did nothing to hide her pretentiousness. My date said nothing throughout the entire exchange.

Phoneymoney: "Oh, no! Is it going to rain? I just bought these shoes. And they weren't cheap.
Unawareman: "Really, how much were they?"
(Unawareman's date makes a sarcastic face at him)
Phoneymoney: "You don't want to know. Let me just say, they probably cost more than that lady's entire outfit." (points to a casually dressed young woman out with her boyfriend).
Unawareman: "Really? Hey I'm curious. Just how much does a pair of shoes like that cost?" (He takes the bait, his date is becoming increasing uncomfortable)
Phoneymoney: "Well, if you are going to harass me all night- they were $280." (smiles smugly at Unawareman's date)
Unawareman: "Oh, that is a lot of money. I hope it doesn't rain on them. Although we could use the rain, my grass is turning brown."
Phoneymoney: (turning to Unawareman's date) "That outfit is sooo cute. Did you get it on sale?"
Unawareman: (to the rescue) "No, I got it as a present for her last birthday."
Phoneymoney: "Really, I've never seen anything like that at Macy's. Or is it from Neiman-Marcus?"
Unawareman: (his date grabs his arm and squeezes, but it's too late.) "No, I got that at JC Penney."
Phoneymoney: "Oh, it doesn't look like it. It's really cute. I got this top at Abercrombie's. It was on sale for $70. I just couldn't pass it up. Of course it's my earrings that really cost too much."

Unawareman: "Are they diamond?" (his date cringes at his foolishness)

Phoneymoney: "They had better be, for what I paid for them! But I just had to have them."

Unawareman: "They look nice. Did you get them in the mall?" (he points to Earring Island)

Phoneymoney: (looking at Unawareman's date) "Honey, where did you find him?"

(Phoneymoney begins to falsely act like "sisters under the skin" as she insults Unawareman's date)

"Please let him know that you do not get earrings like this in the mall. No wonder he thinks you like clothes from JC Penney. You really do need to train this one."

(a false staccato laugh is attempted to disguise the insult as a form of female bonding)

Unawareman: (Unaware that his girlfriend is being insulted in a primitive female way) "She loves JC Penney, but I love Victoria's Secret. It's so expensive. I saw a pair of...."

Phoneymoney: "Tell me about it. However I refuse to buy any of my underwear from anywhere except Victoria's Secret. I only buy the best."

Unawareman: "Well it looks like it is going to rain, do you want...?"

Phoneymoney: "Oh, I just had my hair done. It was so expensive. Do you know how much a ...."

At this point Unawareman's date reaches out and begins to choke Phoneymoney, security is called and the pair is separated.

Phoneymoney: "Oh my God! You crazy bitch! You broke one of my nails! Do you know how much these cost to get done?"

(Unawareman's date lunges forward again, but is stopped)

The first cavewoman that looked down her nose at her next-cave-entrance-over-neighbor for wearing last year's fur may have been responsible for the fashion frenzy of the last 10,000 years. In her defense, it may have been prudent to not wear last year's fur. Fur is the skin of dead animals. The skin was not usually treated with preservatives 10,000 years ago. If it was crudely preserved, the preservatives lasted only a short time before the fur would mold and rot. That first look of disgust may have been one spawned from the smell of rotting animal flesh. But early woman was not known for her communication skills and the look was interpreted by the recipient as "you had better get me new furs so I can shut this bitch up." Wearing last year's "furs" was just not acceptable. Could be the basis for the taboo of wearing last year's fashions? Where did the new furs come from? Why. the hapless caveman, of course. He had to go out, risking life and limb, and kill another animal. More is always better according to the female mindset. Therefore the female cave dweller with the most furs was the most successful at "working" her man. Her children could also be clothed in furs. Matching furs. Color coordinated. Early cavewoman would scoff at others as they walked by in their out-of-fashion furs. We can trace our misery as men back to an early stage in our development. It wasn't long before the females were walking around the cave village with a different fur each day draped over their post simian bodies. Some foolish, enterprising caveman learned how to use animal sinew to connect two animal furs together. He showed his invention to his cave wife and the fashion industry was thrust into the technology age. For centuries after this discovery clothing has marked the status of human beings. This mindset pervades every human society to this day. What started as a practical covering, and hygienic removal of, animal skins from your wives' body has evolved into the multi-billion dollar fashion industry that we see today. Such a mundane topic, but yet it is the heart of the female mindset. Like sheep in a flock, women must dress the same.

Ω

Successful hunting in a cave clan increased their numbers. There was safety in numbers in a primitive society. A successful tribe had successful hunting techniques. Thriving hunters will hunt game that they are successful at killing. The game becomes the staple of the cave clan's diet. The furs become the uniform of the cave clan members. Uniforms evolved. The "Woolly Mammoth People" could be recognized at a distance because the members were wearing Woolly Mammoth furs. This gave the tribe an identity. It also gave the tribe unity. Fashion started out as a need to belong. It is genetically hardwired into our brains to wear similar clothes to the other people in our society. Or in our social class. The wives of the top hunters wore newer, bigger, and nicer furs than the wives of the fat slob that lived on the fringes of the clan. He threw together some beaver furs, a little squirrel skin, and filled in the blank areas with castoff raccoon pelts. His women (wife and daughters) were most likely humiliated to be seen in this fashion garb. Fashion marked early human beings' social class. Fashion became a status symbol. Those with the most furs were held in higher esteem. Esteem in a society, any society, means benefits and privileges. The role of fashion has not changed that much over the centuries. Fashion was used as a status symbol for thousands of years.

Ω

The esteemed of society, throughout history, received more benefits and privileges. Our clothes are linked closely to our roles in society. Status is marked by what we wear. This has been prevalent throughout history. A Russian peasant dressed like a Russian peasant. Russian nobility dressed like Russian nobility. A cave women of low status wore squirrel and raccoon, while the higher status females wore mammoth and saber-toothed tiger. Everyone could see which clan, and which social class within the clan, you belonged to from a distance. Fashion helped people determine that distance. Dirty old clothes–stay back. Clean fashionable clothes – move in for a closer look. A homeless woman and a college coed still send the same signal as their forebears. You walk by one real close and breathe in; the other you walk around and breathe out. Fashion helped people gauge each other as either "threatening or non-threatening" to themselves. Superior or inferior. Dominant or subordinate. These cues were visual and saved a lot of time that was previously spent sniffing each other's asses before stylishness evolved. Tribes in the rain forest adorned themselves according to their identity. The Leaf People wore leaves around their privates. The Feather People wore feathers. This human need to identify with the tribe had a common foundation and was practiced by all peoples of the world. The Mongols of Central Asia wore Mongol attire, and the Masai tribesman of Eastern Africa wore the latest in Masai elegance. Fashion on the outside told everyone who we were on the inside. This worldwide use of fashion persisted for most of human history. It would be hard to mistake a Viking raider from Scandinavia with a Chamorro warrior from Guam.

That is, until Industrial society gave us something called 'leisure time'. Speaking of time, it is time to drink.

Ω

Around the turn of the twentieth century human beings had reached a crossroads in their development. New technologies were making life easier for the average person. New medicines and new surgical techniques enabled people to live longer. The five-day work week gave rise to two days of rest and leisure. This leisure time was unheard of during most of the history of humans. Especially for the working stiff. The average person was more educated and sophisticated than their ancestors. This was a huge change from the previous centuries of human culture. If your father was a blacksmith, you became a blacksmith. As did your son, and his son, and so on for generations. Everyone knew what they were going to do, and what clothes they were going to wear. The Industrial Revolution changed all that. Education and culture was growing upon the previous generations inventions. Life was no longer just a struggle. Pleasure was available for the average person. People could see that there was life outside of the struggle to merely exist. A new concept emerged. The huddled masses now had time on their hands. And money. A "middle" class formed, subverted for centuries, their basic instinct for freedom was being realized. The fence that distinguished peasant and nobility deteriorated. At first, a few boards were lost and some were able to cross over into the others' territory. Then entire sections had been knocked down. Nobles moved away from the peasants. Peasants moved closer to the nobles. The fence was eventually totally removed and the middle ground between the two classes was the area that most of us live in. The class system had changed. No longer were people defined by the black and white lines of social class. Delineated society was replaced with a middle class; a series of gray castes that would ebb and flow with the fortunes of each individual. A class of people; not rulers, yet not truly subjects, emerged around the dust of the trampled fence.

The emergence of a middle class was new to society. As a middle class emerged, it too, became somewhat stratified. The middle class manager made more money than the middle class laborer. They may have lived in the same neighborhood, but they were different. The wife of the middle class manager wore better clothes than the wife of the middle class laborer. In true female nature, she looked down her nose at the wife of the laborer in "last year's furs". But now, the woman at the bottom of the social ladder did not have to dress that way. She could coerce her husband to spend money that was targeted for bills on her clothes. That new dress in the store became the object of all the local woman's desire. The good husband would buy her the dress. She would be the envy of all of the other woman. Clothes were no longer simply functional.

The different jobs in society used different uniforms to best outfit their laborers to withstand the day's rigors. In a factory, the owner dressed differently than the manager. The manager dressed differently than the shift supervisor and the shift supervisor dressed differently than the person doing the actual labor of the industry. You can walk in to any Wal-Mart, and find which people are the cashiers, and which are the mangers simply by observing what they are wearing. Industrial society, at least in the workplace, maintained the uniform for each position. This is true in Wal-Mart. This is also true in every Fortune 500 company in America. The boss dresses better than his subordinates. The mail guy dresses better than the custodian. Uniforms are clear in the workplace. It is true for policeman, fireman, and the military. Uniforms help determine the person that is coming toward you. Cop? Fireman? Marine? Nurse? The uniform is clear.

A person that made sixty dollars each week could spend what they wanted on clothes. Basic needs were being met for most of the population. Although some populations remained in poverty, society as a whole was becoming richer. That sixty dollars covered expenses and left some extra money for entertainment. To buy new furniture. Or home improvements. Maybe a car. Buying clothes beyond their social status was also an option. For the first time in history, a woman could dress outside of her social class. A new dress for the wife was a given. In caveman days, the woman at the bottom of the cave social order was given the least desirable garments. Bitch and moan though she did, her fate was sealed. She was not going to wear any better furs unless she rose in status (which was rare). This uniform marker of social order ruled society for thousands of years. As societies grew, fashions changed. However, the basic premise of fashion stayed the same. Those at the top of the societal ladder wore the most attention-grabbing clothes. Those at the bottom of the ladder wore the most unremarkable clothes. Queen Victoria took hours to get dressed, with the aid of servants. Her subjects, mostly peasants, probably slept in their clothes. But in Industrial society we enter the dawn of a new age. The woman of the family does not have to betray her social status with clothing. She can save some money each week and purchase the clothing of a woman steps above her in the monetary social arena. She can now parade around town in her new outfit. As the other women look at her in admiration, she looks down her nose at them. The arrival of the twentieth century brought with it a fashion industry that has preyed upon woman's insecurities since its inception. The average male, worldwide, spends a considerable percentage of his paycheck on clothing for the women in his life. Mothers, daughters, wives, girlfriends, all require to be adorned in the latest fashion of the day at the expense of their man. All so the woman can look down their nose at other woman. If you have ever seen that, take a long swig.

Women look at other women more than men look at other men. Women do this to rate themselves against the other woman. They usually start with the overall physical attributes of the other women, size, body shape, and general appearance. If the object of their discretion is fat and hairy, they look no further and move on to the next women. This phenomenon happens at every mall. Sit back and watch. A female human being in the mall will not pass by another female human being without checking her out fully. The length of time each woman checks out the other is in direct relation to the appropriateness of the other woman's attire.

If the woman is dressed according to current fashion trends, the other observer may give her a quick glance. The glance says,

> "You are wearing the correct uniform, not too
> showy or revealing. Good job."

She will then move on to the next female. This is usually only done if the female that is being scanned is wearing the correct uniform (not too showy or revealing). The correct uniform has been decided by the fashion industry gurus that are stoned on crack and pot most of the day. And guess what? They are primarily men! And not just gay men, but real men that just happen to like having skinny nineteen year old models undress for them. They love playing with grownup Barbie dolls. But that is not the point. The point is that women are being directed by other women to wear what has been determined through the media as the fashion of the day. And the fashion changes rapidly. Pink is the new black. Black is the new pink. Change happens faster than most women can pay off the credit card charges on the last batch of clothing they purchased. The change happens so fast that it reverts back to previous styles. The seventies look, scoffed at in the eighties made a brief comeback in the late nineties. Why? Because women were told by other women that it was okay to wear the seventies-look clothing. They were scanned, and gratefully acknowledged by other women when they wore the proper clothing. This scanning happens all day in every avenue of life. In the office men meet and talk about the latest trends, where the business is going, who is scoring the big accounts? Women talk about what other women are wearing. No wonder they are less productive than men in the same position. Starting at home, mothers check out daughters, sisters check out sisters. Comments are made as to the closeness of the outfit to what has been prescribed by the fashion industry as "in". As women ride the subway they are scanned and filed by other women based upon their adherence to a strict dress code. Judgments are made- subtly, silently, but made none-theless. Throughout the day, regardless of location, a female is constantly being scanned by other females for her compliance to the dress code. At the end of the day, when women are home with their families, or on the phone with relatives and friends they are talking about the day's fashion information.

"I saw the cutest outfit on the subway today."
Or
"You won't believe what this girl was
weaning; it was so out of style."
Or
"This little slut sat right in front of me, My
God, you could see everything."
Or
"She really dressed well - for her weight."

This is the focus of women's perceptions of other women. It is well known by the fashion industry. They make billions each year by putting out new pieces of cloth, sewn in different ways. They advertise to women that this is what everyone is wearing. Not only direct TV and magazine ads, but they drape their styles over the women that are found on shows that women love, like Sex in the City, and other fantasy shows about "fulfilled" single women. They see what their heroes are wearing and run out to the nearest mall to shop. These mall owners know what type of stores make the most money. Women's apparel. There are 46,512 shopping malls in the United States. If you walk through any of these malls you will find, on the average, that 96% of the stores lean towards women's clothing. So the most numerous of any store in any mall in the United States of America is for women to clothe themselves in the latest fashion as dictated to them by the fashion industry. Women buy clothes at the mall so they can go home and put these clothes on to look good when they go back to the mall to buy more clothes! And the man of the house usually pays for them. If a man does go to the mall he may find some refuge in a Sharper Image store. But the respite is only a brief one as it is on to more stores to look at more styles. The trip from store to store is usually spent checking out the fashions on the other women so the female can pick out the proper uniform for herself. The man of the house gets to carry the bags, and, if he is lucky, sneak a peek through the crack in one of the dressing rooms that women use to try on their clothes. Otherwise his role in the mall is one of function – he is the pack mule for this expensive expedition. The mall is not designed for him to buy anything. Less than four percent of the shops in American malls have stores targeted towards men. Look at the faces of the men and women that are in the mall the next time you visit. The women have direction; the women know where they are going next. They know that they can save money on a clothing item that costs the fashion industry about one dollar to make in a sweatshop overseas. Some of these garments, made by slave labor overseas, are worn to charity events to help the world's poor. Somewhat of an irony, isn't it? These garments made from the sweat and toil of downtrodden third world countries usually price out around 50 times their cost. For the math challenged, that means that a fifty-dollar name brand shirt usually costs the company around a dollar. One buck. Then they mark it down 20% and the women of the house brags that she just saved $10 on a name brand shirt, or dress, or whatever. The man of the house realizes that he dare not interrupt this shopping frenzy with the realization that she did not just save ten dollars; she spent forty dollars! Women would not understand this logic and his torture in the mall would only be prolonged. You see men congregating in the food courts, or on the benches in malls. What are these men doing? Well, that is obvious. They will be ogling the very small percent of women that dress for men.

Ω

Yes, there are women that dress for men. These are women that have been freed from the bonds of sheepdom. These are women that are not trapped in the drone-like existence of the flock of fashion lemmings. These female human beings dress for men. They dress in a way to attract men. They dress to excite men. They dress to accentuate their body. These females are rare. The average male human searches for them constantly. Women that dress for men usually understand men. And they understand women. They understand that women are petty, catty and meander in the illogical all day long. They are not quite at Porn Star status, but they know how to dress for men-usually with clothing that reveals. This could be subtle, blatant, or anywhere in between. The next couple of paragraphs may require you to drink continuously.

I recall one night, many years ago, I was going out with a young woman to a nightclub. She was dressed for the nightclub. Tight black miniskirt, calf-length boots with thigh-high stockings that were barely covered by the miniskirt, a tight blouse with no bra that proudly displayed her nipples and ample cleavage. On our way to the nightclub she wanted to stop at the mall to change her earrings. Since it was just before Christmas the mall was open to 11:00 pm. We stopped in and walked the still crowded mall to the earring store. The stares and looks of disgust were dispensed upon my young date in substantial amounts. Women looked her up and down. Derogatory comments were made loud enough so that she would hear. Adult common females shook their heads and frowned their lips at her. At first my young woman slooped her shoulders, remembering that she was a "bad girl". But then, straightening up, she beamed her beautiful eyes at me. She stuck out her chest, arched her back and inched up her miniskirt, revealing the tops of her thigh highs. Chin up, she strode on. A picture of beauty. A colorful mosaic of black miniskirt, red lipstick and silver eye shadow. Heels clicking as she expressed that she was a woman. She was no longer captive to their stares and criticisms. She was no longer a part of the dismal gray flock. Of course they stared at her. She flaunted her femininity beyond the accepted dress code. And she had the nerve to do it in the highest of all holy places – the Fashion Shrine of the American Mall. It was blasphemy. Even the cashier gasped in disbelief as my date picked out her earrings. Of course, by this time, the men of the late-night mall took notice. Two young men even followed us into the store, pretending to be interested in earrings. Other men were reeled in closely with curt words from their wives; some simply with looks from their mates. One heavily-clad common female hit her husband with her pocketbook for trying to get a peek at the back end of this evolved species of female. My young date had upset the henhouse. Females were clucking everywhere. One overweight common female of particularly nasty disposition even walked up to her and called her a slut. My date's response was to walk down the aisle, turn and smile at this portly common female, and in full view of her two young stalkers, bend over at the waist to pick up a pair of earrings on the bottom tier. The corpulent common female gasped, as the two focused devotees groaned, at the sight.

We walked out of the mall just as eventfully as we came in. The looks and stares of the common females was obtrusive, yet not threatening. My date proudly paraded to the car. When she got to the door she turned to see that her two followers had sauntered out to the parking lot. She turned, smiled, lifted her miniskirt to her waist, and yelled,

"Get a good look, boys."

With that she turned, skirt still held to her waist, and shook her pert little backside at them. The two young men stopped dead in their tracks. Neither said a word throughout the entire episode. They stood there like Bogart on the tarmac as the only real woman they had ever seen beyond the internet stepped into the car and rode away into the night.

Ω

Women dress for women and the fashion industry knows it. If women were to dress for men, they would all be wearing miniskirts and thigh-highs each day. But since the core of a women's sexual strategy is deception - she must play the game of being a good little girl. They think that men will shy away from them if they are too forward. So they all dress the same, wear the same makeup, and act the same. And men, in their desire to appease their mate, accept it. Open another beer and guzzle it.

7

ARE WOMEN ABUSIVE TO MEN?

Appetizer
Chivas Regal Premium Scotch Whiskey

Main Course
Heineken

The abuse of young males begins in our public school system. Energetic young men are subjected to a female dominated school system and subsequently labeled as "disturbed' when they attempt to inquire beyond the teacher's knowledge. This is the beginning of a lifetime of mistreatment that males suffer at the hands of females. Men are also abused in marriage and the media seems to condone this treatment of men. In cases of domestic violence it is the man that usually gets punished-regardless of who was the perpetrator. Since men have been subjected to this mistreatment at such an impressionable age. they begin a lifelong struggle to try and cope with the cruelty heaped upon them by women. Men are murdered by women at higher rates than women are murdered by men. But some men experience a fate worse than death at the hands of their female companion-removal of the penis. All of this abuse starts in kindergarten for young American men.

Schools are for girls. They are designed by women, run by women, and the majority of the teachers are women. From the moment they enter public school boys are targeted for abuse by teachers and female classmates alike. Helpless, innocent young boys can only tolerate this abuse as it is accepted, and nurtured, by a school system that is becoming increasingly male-phobic. This may require a big tug on that beer. Ahhh, here we go.

Public school was designed for females. The male of the species was not programmed to sit still all day. Favoritism notwithstanding, the majority of awards in elementary school are given to the girls. Effeminate boys win a small percentage of the awards only if they submit to their teachers. Until he reaches middle school the American male has only a 9% chance of having a male teacher. And this rate is declining each year. That's right, according to the National Education Association, 91% of elementary school teachers are female. Less and less men are entering teaching due to inadequate pay, social stigma of low status, and the idea that it is "women's work". Men simply do not teach elementary school children. Women have complete control of the academic future of young boys from kindergarten until fifth grade. And young males are targeted early. Young boys are disciplined in schools at a greater rate than females.

United States Department of Education lists approximately 92,000 schools in the United States with an enrollment of 47 million students. The 29,000 private schools enroll over 5 million students. Besides the one percent of students that are home schooled, everyone else goes to public or private school. To teach these students there are approximately 3 million teachers working in public schools, 75 % of whom are female. Eighty-four percent of these teachers are white. White females are teaching our kids. White females do not understand white males, black males, or Hispanic males. They do not understand males at all. From kindergarten to twelfth grade, a male student will spend three-fourths of his academic career in a classroom that is run by a female teacher. And these teachers find ways to take out their wrath on boys. Don't believe me?

Why do more boys than girls end up in special education programs? Small sip here.

According to The Condition of Education 1997, National Center for Education Statistics, U.S. Department of Education, Washington, DC, boys end up in special education classes than girls in the same age group. Looking at the graph that follows, the remarkable numbers are in the area of emotional disturbance.

Ratio of Males to Females Enrolled
in Special Education Programs
Adapted from The Condition of Education 1997, National Center for Education Statistics, 1997, Washington, DC: U.S. Department of Education

Disability	1986	1988	1990	1992
Learning	2:1	2:1	2:1	2:1
Emotional Disturbance	3:1	5:1	3:1	4:1
Mental Retardation	1:1	1:1	1:1	1:1
Total Disabilities	2:1	2:1	2:1	2:1

The elementary teachers, primarily female, label boys as emotionally disturbed at a rate five times more than they label girls as emotionally disturbed. With all else being equal we should see an equal number of girls being labeled as emotionally disturbed. When comparing mentally retarded children the teacher bias fades away. Mentally retarded students are deficient since birth. Unfortunately, retarded children were born that way. They did not need a man-hating female to label them as "behind the group". Nature did that already. In this area of objectivity boys and girls are the same. The groups are in a one to one balance. Nature does not select boys for special education. Women select boys for special education. It is the female centered school system driven by female teachers that disproportionately label boys as deficient. These female teachers do not understand, nor try to understand, the intricacies of the advanced male mind. So they label that which they do not understand as "unfit" or "disabled" and put them in a special class to be ridiculed and cast aside in front of their peers. Within a short time every kid in kindergarten knows which group of kids is the slow group. Female teachers automatically begin to label young boys as "troublesome" or "hyperactive" within days of entering kindergarten. Consider the case of Kyle T., as told by his father:

Kyle was a great kid from the minute he was born. He came out into the world smiling and full of energy. He was a loving kid, very inquisitive of the world. As a baby he did not cry that much. He was so active during the day that he fell right asleep at night. My wife and I both bragged to our friends how Kyle was sleeping through the night by the time he was 3 months old. As he got older he was always on the go. A great kid, full of wonder about the world. He would chase butterflies, and spend fifteen minutes watching the ants build their hill. He started talking when he was 2 years old. By the time he was four he was talking up a storm. He loved to go outside. His favorite place was the zoo. He talked me into getting him a hamster for his fourth birthday. For Christmas he asked Santa for a parakeet. Then came the fish tank his uncle gave him. His room was like a little zoo. By the time he went to kindergarten he knew the names of dozens of animals. I always felt that he would be a veterinarian, or zookeeper, something to do with taking care of animals. He came home from the first day of kindergarten in tears. He had been so excited because he had heard that the teacher had a rabbit. She scolded him, in front of all the other kids when he went to pet the rabbit. I guess she wanted to make an example of him. My wife broke down in tears. I tried to tell her that it was just the first day and everything would be okay as the year went on. The next day he came home upset again. He said that he wasn't going back to school anymore. When I asked why he said that the teacher didn't like him and yelled at him all day. He cry when I said that he had to go to school.

I decided to take the next day off and see how he was doing in school firsthand. I drove him to school and walked him to class. The first thing out of his teacher's mouth was, "Oh, you must be Kyle's dad. So you know what I have to deal with." Taken aback, I resisted the urge to tell her fat ass off. I mean, here is this kid, in his first week of kindergarten, and she already had him pegged as a problem. I had been his dad for over five years at that time and I still was learning something new about him every day; she had spent two half-days with him and was acting like she was an authority on his life. The more I talked to her the less I liked her. She was not an attractive woman, very heavy-obese would be a better description. Real bad acne, couldn't have been more than thirty. As she described Kyle's " problems" I got nauseous. A first I thought I was just another parent in denial. But it kept creeping in on me-this ugly, fat lady has only known my son for a few days and she has already taken a dislike to him. I felt that this was going to be a long year. Then she hit a nerve. She said that "boys like Kyle did well once they were put on medication to help them focus." Boys like Kyle? I reached down and gently grabbed his little hand and turned away from her without saying another word.

My discussion with the principal went nowhere. She made sure that I knew that she was a former kindergarten teacher. She said she knew how difficult some of the boys could be. I was floored. I left with my son, and his future, in my arms. We had a good talk with him that night and he *agreed to go to school the next day. He did okay but I could see his spirit begin to dwindle daily. I did not know what to do. I tried spending even more time with him than before and that seemed to help. He made it through kindergarten and did a little better in first grade. The only time I would see his energetic, inquisitive personality was when he was away from school for awhile. The teachers nagged us for years to put him on medication. We refused to drug our child for being a normal, energetic boy. He finally started to like school when he entered middle school. In sixth grade Kyle had three male teachers and they did fun projects with the kids. He started coming home really excited about school. What a relief. He had male teachers in high school and he did very well. It was a shame that the women teachers he had were so "against" him (hands held in air with two fingers making quotation marks). They all seemed to fit the same mold-not married, not attractive, no kids, significantly overweight, anti-boy. Those elementary years were the toughest years of our lives – both me and him. I am glad that it is over.*

He is seventeen now, plays the piano and the guitar, speaks fluent French, and has just been accepted to the University of Miami pre-med program. He still loves the outdoors and has a room full of lizards and snakes. I think he did alright in spite of the unqualified, sexist teachers he had in his early years.

The story of Kyle is one that ends well. But his outcome is rare. Many parents will accept the school's diagnosis of their child. Young boys that are active and like to explore seem to be a particular target for the female teacher. Her simple mind does not understand exploration so it decides that it is insubordination. The overriding desire that has propelled men to seek out new lands, discover exotic places on Earth, land on the moon, and shoot spacecraft out of our solar system is a primary function of the male brain.

The female teacher does not possess these faculties. Females did not discover America, the Titanic, or land a man on the moon. These were the results of the superior male mind. A female teacher understands simple tasks. Like sitting down in your seat quietly. Like listening to the teacher drone on and on about adjectives and prepositions and verbs. Boys have a difficult time quelling their inquisitive mind during these boring lectures. This upsets the female teacher. She must get these errant boys into line. She may even have a history of being "wronged" by men. When you add this resentment to the equation you have a formula for methodical revenge on the male species.

I have over twenty years of experience in the public school system. I taught middle and high school science during my years in the classroom. As an administrator I have experience at all three levels; elementary, middle, and high school. The research substantiates my own experiences.. When I became an Assistant Principal for Discipline I saw a true picture of how female teachers treated their students, particularly males. There appears to be an abundance of young men sent out of the classroom by female teachers. Why? If you have ever been embarrassed by a female teacher you are allowed to drink the rest of your beer and open another.

There have been quite a few gender equity studies over the last four decades. One study, by the American Association of University Women (AAUW), conducted between 1990 and 1991 seems to hint that there may be a bias towards males in our school system. The AAUW report attributes this discrepancy to school bias: teachers discriminate against badly-behaved boys. Mislabeling boys may indeed be part of the explanation. But many of these disabilities appear long before boys even enter school.

Most students believe that teachers pay more attention to girls, call on girls more often, and give praise to girls more frequently than boys. They also believe that boys are disciplined more regularly than girls, and sent to the office more than girls. Drink and read the chart.

Adapted from Expectations and Aspirations: Gender Roles and Self-Esteem, by AAUW/Greenberg-Lake, 1990, Washington, DC: Greenberg-Lake.

Student Beliefs	Boys' Perceptions	Girls' Perceptions
Who does the teacher call on more often in class?		
Boys	36%	35%
Girls	59%	57%
Who does the teacher pay more attention to in class?		
Boys	29%	33%
Girls	64%	57%

Boys mature more slowly than girls. The male brain, being more complex, takes a little longer to set down the neuronal path to greatness. This characteristic is exploited by the female dominated school system to label boys as poor learners and assigned to slower groups and cast into low ability groups where they are set apart from the rest of the class during the elementary grades. This impacts the self esteem of the isolated individuals.

Student Beliefs	Boys' Responses	Girls' Responses
Who does the teacher think is a better student?		
Boys	26%	13%
Girls	69%	81%
Who does the teacher compliment more often in class?		
Boys	15%	7%
Girls	81%	89%

Teachers punish boys more often. This makes sense since the majority of teachers are women. When a women sees a young girl misbehaving she does not feel threatened, she sees this a typical girl behavior. The teacher may have even done the same thing when she was in school.

But when a boy misbehaves the teacher, seventy-five per-cent of which are female, do not relate to this behavior, feel threatened or disrespected, and report the boy to the admin-istration.

Student Beliefs		
Who does the teacher punish more often in class?	Boys' Responses	Girls' Responses
Boys	90%	92%
Girls	8%	5%
Who does the teacher like to be around more in class?		
Boys	21%	27%
Girls	73%	80%

In the four years while I was an assistant principal for discipline at a rural K-8 school in central Florida I handled 5,312 discipline referrals. Schools keep good records. A discipline referral is written when a teacher has tried everything that she knows to get a student to behave in her class-and fails. I have this number because I kept records of every student that was sent to my office. This allowed me to spot trends. I was able to sort discipline referrals each year by time, date, incident type, teacher, grade level, age of student, and sex of student. Yes, I could tell the numbers of boys that were sent as opposed to the number of girls that were sent to the office. The difference was remarkable. Of the 5,312 discipline referrals that I personally handled, 5,018 were written on boys. The difference, for the mathematicians that are out there, is 294. That means that only 294 girls were sent to the office on discipline referrals. It is obvious that the system does not allow for male expression. Male human beings are not built to sit down and listen to woman drone on and on about mundane topics. They are built to explore the world. To seek out new lives and civilizations. To boldly go where no man has gone before. Female teachers do not understand the male psyche. When one of these young males decides to give in to his basal male instincts and explore – he is quickly disciplined. Female teachers, on the whole, spend a majority of their classroom discipline attempting to quell the basic instincts of young boys. Most of the referrals that were written on boys were written for incidents that are biologically-programmed male traits. These traits are attacked daily by the thousands of female teachers across America. Young girls, on the other hand are routinely allowed to engage in traditionally female pastimes; note passing, chatting with their female friends, as well as putting on makeup. The public school system is a great emasculator. It starts in kindergarten and continues until young men are forced to wear "gowns" as they walk down the aisle towards graduation.

During my tenure as an assistant principal I witnessed many incidents of students hitting other students. The female students would routinely hit the male students. This was rarely reported by teachers. Of the few incidents that females were reported for hitting it was usually not written down on a discipline referral. The teacher would send the female up to the office with a note saying that the young girl had kicked a boy - but he deserved it. In subsequent conversations with the teacher she would usually say that she had only sent the girl to the office to "cover herself" in case the parents' of the young boy that was assaulted called the school to complain. Of the 1,237 discipline referrals that were written for hitting in four years, only two were written on female students. Our school policy was to send students home when they hit other students out of anger. This greatly reduced the number of kids that hit other kids. Both of these girls' parents refused to accept my explanation as to why the girls were being sent home for the rest of the day. Both sets of parents were adamant that the boy that was hit "deserved it". I remember one very clearly. The young lady was sent to me office for hitting a male class-mate. She admitted to hitting him. According to our school policy, I called the young lady's home to have the parent come to school and pick up their daughter. A female answered the phone (Names have been changed to protect the innocent).

"Hello."
"Good afternoon ma'am. This is Mr. O'Cahir, assistant principal for discipline at Susan B. Anthony Public School. Is this the parent of Lacey Underall?"
"Yes, is everything okay? Has my daughter been hurt?"
"No, ma'am your daughter has not been injured at all. She is fine. As a matter of fact she is sitting right here. The reason I am calling is that she has been sent to the office for hitting another student. In order to reduce the incidents of hitting our school policy has been to send the offending student home on that day in lieu of a one-day suspension. Can you pick up your daughter from school?"
"Oh my God! She hit someone? And she is being suspended? Oh, no!"
"Actually, she is being sent home for the rest of the day. She will only be suspended if you cannot pick her up."
"Oh. Can I talk to her?" I agreed and handed the phone to Lacey. She cried real tears immediately. I could hear her mother chiding her loudly for hitting another student. I could actually hear the shrill voice Lacey's mom asking her who it was that she hit.
"Phillip. He said I was fat." I heard a loud scream on the other end and Lacey pulled the phone away from her ear, her face contorted in aural pain.
"LET ME SPEAK TO MR. O'CAHIR!" came screeching through the ear piece like a tin record that had the needle pulled across it. I reached for the receiver.
"Yes, ma'am."

And she let me have it. Oh, boy did she give me a piece of her mind. How unfair I was, how Phillip had said stuff to her daughter in the past, how she was going to the school board about me. As an assistant principal, I had heard it before so I stood my ground. She came down to school and picked up her daughter later that afternoon. She once again let go a tirade on me as to how Phillip deserved it and so on and so on. Rising from her seat she straightened her composure and faced me, with her daughter by her side.

"I am going to say it in front of you, Mr. O'Cahir. So you know where it came from."

I stared through her. I knew what she was going to say next but I let her continue. People have an innate desire to be heard, and I did not want to suppress that. They also have an intrinsic need to be their child's "hero". I knew that she would say something that would show her daughter that she had no respect for my decision to send her home. This usually put the parent in the position of saying the wrong thing. The positive part is that when they say the wrong thing I am spared a phone call to the school board. They play their trump card by telling me off. It's just part of the job of being an assistant principal for discipline. She faced Lacey and gripped her by the shoulders, looking into her eyes.

"If Phillip, or any other boy, calls you any name whatsoever, I want you to kick him square between the legs. Make it worth being sent home."

Mechanically turning her head to me she took aim, and fired, with cold steely eyes.

"Have a good day, Mr. O'Cahir."

She strode meaningfully forward with her right foot, cocking her chin toward the ceiling and walking away with her head held at the forty-five degree angle of mammalian defiance. She had a right. The torch was passed to a new generation of females. Let the word go forth that a fresh generation of American females had the right to hit men for whatever reason they desired. The other female that was written up gave similar excuses for hitting the boy. I sent her home with similar protests.

Looking back I realize that I was part of this problem. I would see girls' kicking boys in the shins and give them a verbal warning. When I saw a boy doing the same thing, I sent him home. I had been conditioned by the same system that I was representing. Boys are not allowed to hit girls, but girls can hit boys all that they want. The acceptance of females hitting males starts in our public school system.

There are no statistics for the emotional abuse that woman direct toward men. There is only the personal experience, and pain, of millions of men. There is no "Men's Hurt Feelings Hotline", or a "Nationwide Study of the Statistics of Emotional Damage to Men". Nor will there be any statistics taken on the emotional pain that women cause men. What I am about to impart comes from hundreds of conversations with men over a thirty year period.

As stated earlier women begin to harass and emotionally abuse men at a young age, around the time that both sexes enter middle school. Sometimes it is sooner, but middle school is usually prime time for the female of our species to begin its quest. It is in the region of the sixth grade that both sexes teeter on the precipice of entering puberty. Some kids have already fallen in the puberty chasm, while others may stay on the edge of childhood for a few more years. Young men usually lag behind young women in sexual development. While their bodies may lag behind their tender emotions do not. You see, young boys are taught not to cry. You scrape your knee and are told to take it like a man. Men are looked upon with disdain if they cry when they experience physical pain. Boys don't cry. There may be some Darwinian explanation as to why girls hit boys so often. Maybe they are trying to see which male can withstand the most abuse, kind of like a test for the future abuses that men will ultimately face at the hands of women during marriage (but let's not get too far ahead of ourselves). Anyway, from kindergarten through high school boys are scolded when they cry, told to "suck it up' when experiencing pain, and praised for being stoic while their body cries out in agony. By the time a young man reaches the sixth grade he knows the rules. Boys don't cry when experiencing physical pain. Crybabies are not what we want. The mold is set, and for most men, the die is cast. Then comes sixth grade. And girls. About two thirds of the girls developed over the summer. Some came into menses, others grew breasts. Less than one quarter of the boys hit puberty. Some grow a little pubic hair, others experience their voice deepening- the classic symptoms. That leaves a big discrepancy developmentally between the sexes. Most of the young ladies are coming into the new school year with a different body. Only a few of the boys are coming into the "game" with new equipment. The majority of young lads are coming into this new environment with the same mindset that they had last year. Dumb boy stuff. The girls have been plotting and planning all summer. Reading teen magazines about love and boyfriends. Stories of how to put on makeup, accessorize their earrings with their purse, how to kiss, and how to catch the eye of the male of the species. The boys played baseball, kickball, built forts, caught frogs, and maybe looked at their older brother's Playboy magazine. Maybe. Like cows being funneled down the runway of the slaughterhouse, the young men bustle in to sixth grade unprepared mentally for the emotional angst that is about to come their way. Pencils, pens, books and mean teachers are the least of their troubles. As the curriculum attempts to prepare the student for survival in the outside world, the female of the species has her own curriculum. One of selection. They are mere children, driven by an onset of hormones, and influenced by a society that says it is okay to hurt men's feelings. It is not only acceptable, it is commendable. A badge of honor to reject suitors. Women exploit this aberration of society. She begins at an early age defining what a "real" man should do. While the poor young man, barely influenced by the testosterone-induced sex drive that will permeate his views for the remainder of his life, attempts to please this female, she is already exploiting his basic need for sex. She is manipulating him for her own ends by telling him how to behave in order to win her favor. He will bring flowers. He will buy presents. Send her love notes. She will meet with her girlfriends to give a full report of his efforts numerous times each day. He has hopes that she will be his "girlfriend". To him a girl friend is as loyal as his male friends. He quickly finds out the truth of female loyalty. His optimism will be dashed before the month is out. The average length of a middle school relationship is two weeks. The young lady usually terminates the relationship. She doesn't want a relationship. She wants to be pursued. After the relationship is over, she will sell him out to her friends as not worthy, picking apart his every flaw. This is the training ground that all females go through to prepare for marriage. One day her husband will be the object of her derision. He will not get off as easy. He will be stuck emotionally, and financially, in the relationship. After a while she will want to be pursued again. The husband is out in the cold. He cannot compete with the exciting Mr. New Guy. No wife, no kids, no money. Let's not get ahead of ourselves.

Or get sober. Suck down a long swallow.

Women begin their attacks on men at a very young age and continue well into their senior years. Men continue to be a slave to woman into their high school years. Testosterone chains them like slaves to the female of their liking. They are easily aroused. As a young man I remember hearing the word, "exotic" spoken by an attractive English teacher I had- causing an erection for the rest of the class. I knew that "exotic" did not mean "erotic" but my pecker did not. My member made no selection between the inflection from the direction of sexual connection and developed into an erection. That is very common in high school boys. The least bit of stimuli to the penile area – and it is hard. The drive is unbelievable. It is amazing that men are as controlled as they are considering the power of the male sex dive. High school girls know this and love it. They actually love the power that they have over "it". For the first time in their lives, they are in charge of something. Up until this point, they had to accede to their fathers, uncles, or even boys on the playground, especially when it came to physical contests. Now they could keep this male in a sexual stupor for days, maybe even weeks. Men are slaves to the male sex drive. Teenage girls realize this very early. They commence to exploit it to the detriment of their male colleagues almost as soon as they learn it.

Ω

Females use male pursuit for their own sense of worth as adolescents. The more men that the young lady can say are chasing her-the more she is envied by her friends. Young female teenagers on a sleep-over talk about what young males will do for them. It is a badge of honor. The discussion will soon twist to the undying love that these young men have shown for the young girls. Real or imagined. This gives the female a sense of supremacy. Sex is nice, but the feeling of power over another human being is basic to the genetics of all societal progression. Women feel this power at a young age. People that enjoy power do not want to lose that power. Sometimes this power finds itself in wrong hands. Consider the story about Stevie L., as related by his best friend. Both are high school students from the Midwest.

At first I felt good for Stevie. He started dating Rhonda H., I mean she was the absolute hottest chick in school. Great tits, nice ass, beautiful face. Man, she had it all. But, like, she knew it. I think that was what made her so sexy. She was confident about her looks when other girls were insecure. I mean, high school girls get a pimple and they are absent from school for a week. But Rhonda just didn't seem to care. She just oozed sex. Stevie really dug her. She was dating a guy that had graduated when he met her. The guy was in college in New Jersey-about six hours away. At first Stevie and Rhonda started just hanging out together.

Then you saw them everywhere. I knew Stevie was hooked. We had been friends since the fourth grade. He was in love. One night they got drunk and had sex. After that Stevie was smitten. She led him around like a puppy, telling him to get her a Pepsi, or" go get my lunch for me". Stevie just did what she said. It got worse as time went on. He was like her personal servant. We all started to notice a big change in him. He would drink a lot when she was around. He always had to get her alcohol.

He would kiss her ass while she treated him like he was furniture. Curious, as friends are, I asked how often he had done her. He said that she only let him do it three times. Three times? He had been seeing her for five months, brought her flowers weekly, and they only had sex THREE TIMES! Most kids I know would do it three times in a night! She was playing him for a sucker. One weekend her "ex" boyfriend came home. She spent the whole weekend with him. I saw Stevie at a party and he was drunk. He looked like he had been crying. I tried to talk to him but he stormed off. Later on that week he told me that she said she had "gotten together" with her "ex" a few times during the weekend. Stevie was devastated. She continued to lead him around during the week, Stevie kept buying her stuff, she was really doing a number on him. About every other weekend the "ex" would come home. Stevie would get drunk. She would admit to him that they had "gotten to-gether" – which broke Stevie's heart. Man, I really started to hate that bitch. One time I confronted her and she just said that I wished that I had it so good. Last month Stevie took a whole bunch of pills and they found him unconscious in the boys' restroom at the football field. They pumped his stomach. He made it - but the next weekend he was back kissing her ass at a party at the lake. She was flirting with everyone. The "ex" showed up and kicked Stevie's ass. We had to break it up. Then she leaves with the asshole!

Stevie is a mess. I wish she would stop screwing with him. She knows the hold she has over him and works it just to have someone kissing her ass while her boyfriend is away.

There are many groundless beliefs that saturate society regarding relationships between a man and a woman. That somehow before, during, or after, the breakup of a relationship between a man and a woman, it is usually the man who is at fault. One common divorce saga is that the ex-wife was in some way "abused" or "neglected" by the husband. The blame for the divorce is usually attributed to the husband. People say that he "couldn't keep her happy", or "he failed to keep his family together". Moreover, it is usually a stereotypical, testosterone-based form of abuse that causes the woman to be justified in her sacred mission to release herself from this violent, domineering monster. In fact, frequently the opposite is true. Overall women are more physically and emotionally abusive to men than men are to women. Although widely underreported, a majority of domestic violence victims are men. But men do not whine and call the police every time their wives hit them or emotionally abuses them. They try to solve the problem themselves. Domestic violence is not a phenomenon of the emotionally distraught women finally saying she has "had enough". That is the fairy tale accepted by a society in which 'male bashing' is the daily pastime. Starting at a young age society conditions women to abuse men both physically and emotionally. This behavior begins when young boys and girls first enter the female dominated public school arena. There have been hundreds of studies on domestic violence in the last forty years. Just about every sociology major that could not find a job applies for a grant to study the causes of domestic violence in America. The stereotypical scenario is that of the helpless wife that is being used as a punching bag by her impotent, unemployed, alcoholic husband. The husband is categorized as a bully that cannot succeed in a man's world. So he beats up his poor defenseless wife. And the wife, stoically, selflessly, takes it for years. For the kids. For love. Because she feels her husband's pain on a deeper level. She is better than him. She is a strong wonderful person that has vowed to stay with this loser for better or for worse. Or consider the classic Hollywood scenario; she cannot leave because she is from an abused household and that is all she knows. The black eyes, the bruises, the verbal abuse, emotional neglect, it is all part of what she has accepted as her lot. There is even a T-shirt named after the battering husband: 'The Wife Beater'. Funny thing is, according to statistics, the stereotype is not the norm. Not even close. The statistics show that this scenario is less than 2 % of all domestic abuse cases. What does that leave? 98%? 98% of the cases of domestic abuse do not involve the helpless female being assaulted by the impotent, unemployed, alcoholic husband. Ninety-eight percent is pretty close to just about every case. In fact, over half of the reported cases of domestic violence are committed by woman. This is corroborated by a study done by Bruce Heady and Dorothy Scott of Melbourne University on domestic violence. Collectively these studies show a decline by 50% in male-perpetrated acts during the last ten years. A decline. Once again men are learning from the past and improving their behavior for the betterment of society. The amount of female perpetrated acts of violence actually rose by 37%. An increase. And even this statistic is skewed. Men simply do not call the police when their wives, or girlfriends, hit them. They too have become acclimated to the notion that men are to be hit by women without retaliation. It was all those years of brainwashing that took place in the public school system.

The "Violence Against Women Act" of 1993 stood in stark contrast to the increasing tendency of women to commit "violence against men." Violence studies showed time after time that it was the male who was consistently abused in domestic situations. But this iniquitous act gave women even more impunity to beat the shit out of their husbands, while the men suffered a loss of legal rights as guaranteed by the Constitution of the United States. One of these rights that were suspended because of the "Violence Against Women Act" is the right of the male to obtain counsel and avoid incarceration until he is proven guilty. Basically the law states that if the woman says he did it, he did it. No rights, no hearing, he is guilty until proven innocent (proven innocent-which rarely happens). This happens not only in criminal court; but in the court of "public opinion". His innocence is never proven. According to national arrest statistics, men constitute 92% of the arrests in domestic assault cases. But yet women hit men 52 % more times than men hit women. In only 8% of the arrests are woman hauled off to jail. Here is where the statistics get even more interesting. Of the 8% of woman that get arrested for domestic violence, 86 % are found to be overweight by forty or more pounds. Thin, good looking woman are not being arrested,. The fat, ugly ones get hauled off to jail with statistical regularity. Hmmm.

We cannot continue in this discussion until we look at the influence that society has on our young people. When I say "society", I am referring directly to the mainstream media. Television, music, radio, and magazines have become our society. It is how we transmit our information. We have left the traditional values and great works for the quick fix of the day. We look for the thrill of the moment. We are constantly seeking new stimulation. What is more stimulating than the Battle of the Sexes? The 1970's television show, Sonny and Cher, is a good example. Women loved the show. It was very successful for years. Sonny was consistently berated by Cher on the show. She would make quips about his manhood, his singing ability, and his plans for the future, just about everything the guy did was subject to sarcasm by Cher. Now I love Cher, don't get me wrong. She is a great actress, singer, and is one 'Real Woman' if there ever was one. But during the Sonny and Cher Show she set the tone for the next thirty years where females berated and verbally abused males in order to get higher ratings for their show. I challenge the reader to obtain the old Sonny and Cher Show, it must be on DVD somewhere, and find one episode in which Sonny is not the target of Cher's abuse. It doesn't exist. (In spite of all his alleged shortcomings, Sonny Bono went on to become a respected Congressman and politician.) So we have many homebound housewives, inherently unhappy, influencing the ratings of the major television networks. Television shows only make money if people watch them. And the main viewing audience in the 1960's, especially in the daytime, consisted of housewives. It is through the influence of television that the male of our species has become a punching bag in society today. The ingredients for disaster are already in the pot. Let's see the dish we have concocted when we heat and stir this mix over the next thirty years.

Have you watched television in the last ten years? Of course you have. One of the more popular shows of the last ten years is a situation comedy called "Seinfeld". Anyone that watches "Seinfeld" can see how acceptable female to male violence is in our society. In almost every episode Elaine Bennis, the aging spinster on the show, whacks, pushes, slaps, punches, clouts, or somehow strikes a male member of the cast. In most cases she hits so violently as to cause the hapless victim to fall down. And everyone laughs. She is barely able to have a conversation with any-one that stands within striking distance without hitting them. And it is all in the name of comedy. Elaine is ap-plauded as she rips a toupee off one cast members head, cuts the ponytail off a sleeping male (because he wouldn't give her a discount on a dress) and runs violently amok against any male that crosses her path. I love to watch Sein-feld. It is a funny show. Even the reruns are funny. But the violence that Elaine performs against the male is vicious. Could you imagine ripping the wig off of a female in pub-lic? You would be ostracized by everyone that knew you. If a girl does it – everyone laughs. If a guy wears a wig to hide his baldness he is to be ridiculed and made fun of. If a female wears a wig to hide her baldness (3% of the adult female population goes bald) she is to be pitied and sympa-thized with. Does that look like a double standard? Could you imagine cutting off the ponytail of a sleeping female? You would be arrested, and then detested by everyone that knew you. But if a female does the exact same thing, it is considered hilarious. Go figure. Seinfeld is not the only tel-evision show that uses female against male violence as a comedy backdrop. The leading men in television are habit-ually bumbling idiots From Al Bundy of Married With Children to Ralph Cramden of The Honeymooners; throw in a Homer Simpson, or two, and you have the average week of American television.

Now who do you think is writing these episodes? It is a fact that over 87% of television writers are men. Yes, men are putting men in a dim light. To once again appeal to women. Women are the ones that pick out the products the family uses. She is the one with the time to stay home and discern which toothpaste to buy, which cell phone has the best plan. Even if she doesn't she will say that she does.

Take some time to watch how men are portrayed in television advertisements. Usually the father is pasty-faced, pudgy, balding 30ish squat bodies that cannot seem to get out of their own way. That is, if he is white. If he is black or Hispanic, he is loud, boisterous, and stereotypical old-school minority. It is rare to see an adult human male portrayed on television commercials as anything less than a moronic pain in the ass. Men on television are usually not sexually appealing. And the question you ask is why? Why are men portraying other men this way? Is it to bolster themselves (the writers) as above the norm? To fill in for a weak ego by making other men look like idiots? Not really. Male advertising writers will tell you that the majority of their viewers are women. If the women can relate to even a tiny fraction of the disgusting person they are depicting as the father of the family they will increase the sales of the product. She can rationalize that this male on television is a bigger dope than her husband. Why should she feel bad about her husband when she could have one of these losers to come home to. Subtle psychology on the unhappy female mind. Advertising executives know how miserable women are. They also know that the subtle feeling of satisfaction that a woman feels when she sees an advertisement that illustrates men as helpless will stay in her subconscious mind. It is really the Cave Harlot in them trying to justify an affair. At the supermarket the subconscious mind will scream out "BUY IT!" when the brainwashed female cruises past the advertised product. It appealed to her sexual strategy of having one man take care of her while she bangs another. So men are not selling out men by giving a pudgy, pasty picture of men. Men are selling products to women, which is very easy to do. The male advertising executive knows that it doesn't matter what women think of men- just that they think of men while they shop.

Ω

Gone are the good old days when women who murder their husbands are put to death for their crime. Today they are made into heroes on the six o'clock news, or, if they are lucky, Hollywood movies. Consider the case of Ruth Brown Snyder. Ruth's husband Albert was the art editor at Motor Boating magazine and left poor Ruth home alone each day. Ruth had been having extramarital trysts with her lover, Judd Gray, for two years. The pair had been meeting in seedy hotels for their lurid liaisons when Ruth's daughter was home. At times, they would even bring the young girl to the hotel and leave her in the lobby while they went upstairs to fornicate madly. If the Snyder child was at school the pair would meet at Ruth's home for their wicked rendezvous. Ruth lived well on Albert's salary while having sex with her lover during the day. Not happy with things the way they were, Ruth had persuaded her husband to take out a $48,000 life insurance policy and then planned his demise. Ruth attempted to poison her husband in a variety of ways. The knockout drops Ruth put in her husband's drinks only served to put him in a stupor until they wore off. Ruth persisted with various doses of sleeping powders, but to no avail. Ruth also tried to poison him with rat poison as a cure for the hiccups. This just made poor Albert Snyder very ill for a few days. Frustrated, Ruth then enlisted the help of her lover in her dastardly scheme. At first Judd Gray steadfastly refused. But after months of threats and coercions he gave in.

Judd Gray let himself into the familiar house of Albert Snyder on Saturday, March 19, 1927 while the Snyder family was attending a party. The Snyder's returned around 2:00 a.m. and everyone went to bed except for Ruth Snyder. She took off all of her clothes except for a slip, found her lover in the spare room that he was hiding in, and had sex with him while her husband and daughter nestled in slumber just down the hall. After the lovemaking, Ruth gathered up the murder weapons. Having failed so many times, she was leaving nothing to chance this time. She had gathered together a solid iron window weight, rubber gloves, and chloroform. Ruth handed the heavy metal weight to Gray and tread precariously towards her husband's room. Gray hit the sleeping victim on the head but struck a glancing blow waking up Albert Snyder. Realizing what was happening, Albert Snyder grabbed the intruder by the throat and strangled him. The struggle tore loose Gray's tie pin and it landed on the floor. Gray dropped the weight and let out a whining scream. Judd Gray was almost overpowered when Ruth Snyder intervened. Ruth Snyder became enraged at Gray's ineptness, picked up the weight, and bashed in her dazed husband's skull, killing him. Ruth finally succeeded after various attempts to kill her husband had failed. After they recovered. the murderous couple tied a wire around Albert Snyder's neck before stuffing his nose full of rags that had been soaked in chloroform. The duo then tried to make it look as if there had been a robbery in the house. Ruth hid her valuables around the house to make it appear as if they were missing. Gray then set about to tearing up the house to make it look like a real authentic down home break-in. Gray tied up Ruth Snyder, hid the murder weapon in the basement and left the house.

Ruth Snyder, her maternal instincts notwithstanding, knocked around until she awoke her daughter and sent the youth to the neighbor's house to call the police. The story began to unravel almost immediately. When the police found all of the "missing" loot, the couple broke down. The key piece of evidence that was found by police was the tie pin that had been knocked loose by Mr. Snyder as he fought for his life. Good detective work and tireless police questioning shot the couples story full of holes. They both confessed after being caught in lie after lie. The crime was the media event of the day. Celebrities and dignitaries alike crowded into the small courtroom. The lovers were tried together, found guilty together, and executed within minutes of each other. Could anyone imagine what would happen in today's society?

In today's society Ruth Snyder would first claim that she was the victim of abuse. Before the facts of the case were released the various women's rights groups would be in the street protesting her innocence and demanding her release. Her husband would be tried, and convicted, of being whatever Ruth said he was in the court of public opinion. His reputation would be destroyed as the media bombarded the populace with stories of abuse, torrid sexual affairs, wild drug parties, or whatever else Ruth decided to fabricate in her defense. A man's life would be held up for scrutiny solely on the word of his murderer.

Ruth Snyder would be tried in a kangaroo court, found innocent, and given the attention and sympathy of a society that has been conditioned to think that men are expendable, especially if their wife says she was abused. Then she has every right to kill him.

"*I love you to death.*" It is a comedy about a woman that tries to kill her husband. Here's the ironic part- it was based on a true story. According to FBI statistics, women outpace men in spousal homicide by a ratio of 4:1. Men also suffer a higher rate of multiple offender killings. This is where a "contract" is put on her ex-husband and she coerces her new boyfriend to kill him.

Ω

For good measure, let's add a pair of testicles to the broth.

Kicking a man in testicles really hurts the man. Believe me. I can speak for the entire male population on this one. Every man that has a pair of nuts has been kicked there. Most of this kicking has been done by females. This is not a natural behavior. It has been encouraged by the media since the 1960's. It was acceptable and liberating humor on many drive-in movies during the 1960's. The situation usually called for the female to be justified in her abuse of the male's gonads. It was always viewed as funny. The man did not grimace in pain as much as he displayed a face of shocked resignation. He even acted like he deserved it. Upon recovering he would walk alongside his attacker with submissive resignation. This behavior soon infiltrated on to the television. It brainwashed young girls that it was okay, even expected, to kick a young man in the testicles if he said the wrong thing. The twisted tree of political correctness was beginning to take root. In this case it was accepting an agonizing kick in the scrotum.

Is there a female counterpart to this behavior? Not even close. See how far they bury you in jail if you even attempt to kick a female in the crotch. Consider the man that gets kicked in the nuts and reflexively slaps his female attacker in the face. He's going to jail. At best, he is going to be whipped with a branch from the politically correctness tree. He has no right to strike a female.

Attacking the male genitals has made its way to children's shows. While it is still considered inappropriate for a children's show to foster the situation in which a man deserves to be kicked in the nuts, the nuts still fall victim to attack. Children's movies and television shows routinely show grown men being hit, barreled, and pummeled by objects to the groin. After viewing "Home Alone" I was aghast at the reaction of the children in the crowd when the villains take a bucket of paint in the testicles. They laughed harder than the parts about farting. There was no care to the pain the man was feeling. He had the shocked look of accepting disbelief that is the trademark of the Hollywood nutcracker. Ah, the good ol' days, when farts were funny and a man's gonads were sacred ground. Both the penis and the testicles may suffer irreversible damage. Better have a beer.

Damage to the penis can result in Peyronie's Disease. This is a curvature of the penis due to blunt trauma. The penis curves in the direction of the damaged tissue. There is no cure. The cells of the penis are so specialized that they cannot regenerate themselves when severely injured. In extreme cases an erection is so painful that intercourse is very uncomfortable, maybe even impossible. In mild cases the man has to live with the stigma of a curved penis. There are many men that have curved members as a result of being kicked in the penis hard. A friend of mine was nicknamed "Banana Dick" by his spiteful ex-girlfriend. This lifelong deformity is laughed at by females. Abuse? She kicks you in the penis for no valid reason, your dick is permanently deformed, and she thinks it is funny.

Say that to any female. You pick one. Tell her that if you kick a guy in the dick it could permanently cause his pecker to bend unnaturally when he gets an erection. I will send you money if she doesn't at least smile. Most will laugh. Women are conditioned to abuse men. The conditioning is complete when she damages a man's most prized possession.

Equity? Ted Bundy cut off the nipples of some of his victims. When a female relates that tidbit to a male he reflexively moves his hands to his own nipples, recoiling in horror. He can relate. He has nipples. Women do not relate to the pain a man feels when kicked in the privates. In their feeble minds there is no pain. They do not understand men. How could one try to even surmise that they would understand a man's pain? The damage a direct shot to the testicles may cause is even greater. Some women go even further to vent their frustration of not owning a penis.

According to Violence Researcher Suzanne Steinmetz of Indiana University, "husband beating" is the most unreported crime in the United States. According to one study, women admitted committing severe aggression at three times the rate of men. Throwing objects, kicking and slapping are common examples of women's aggression towards men. But this physical abuse pales in comparison to the emotional abuse that women subject men to. Locking their husband out of the house, hiding his car keys, perpetuating a stressful atmosphere in front of the children, denying the husband sex, stating or insinuating that the husband does not satisfy her sexually, arguing with his every statement, public disrespect - the list goes on and on.

Women still smile when they hear of Lorena Bobbit, the psychotic sociopath that cut off her husband's penis as he slept. What happened to Ms. Bobbit for bobbing it? Is she still in prison? Did she do hard time? Not a chance. She was sentenced to forty-five days in a psychiatric hospital. The judge said that she was "under duress" which caused her to become "temporarily insane". Therefore, she was not liable for the damage to her husband's penis. Gee, what a defense. What do you think would have happened to her husband if he cut off one of her clitoris? This is a bizarre example, but stay with me a minute. Cutting off someone's clitoris is wrong, as is cutting off any body part of any human being. If a man did this to a woman; he would be in jail to this day. Men go to jail for feeling up a women- never mind severing something. Most people think that the Lorena Bobbit case is a rarity. Consider the following real life examples.

> March 2006 - Avelina Rule hacks off the penis of her husband with a machete. She reported that he had insulted her by asking for sex during the daytime.

> July 2005 -Delmy Ruiz, 49, severed Armando Nunez's penis with a knife while he was sleeping. 80% of Nunez' penis was removed by Delmy Ruiz, leaving only a nub. Her motive was jealousy. Ms. Ruiz served a short prison sentence and was released. The penis

was never recovered because Ruiz' dog re moved it from the scene.(man's best friend?)

> February 2005 – Kim Tran severed her boy friend's penis with a kitchen knife. The severed organ was flushed down the toilet but retrieved and later successfully reattached. Charges of sexual assault were dropped. Ms. Tran was convicted of assault with a weapon and received a short prison sentence. Ms. Tran had tricked her boyfriend into being tied up for kinky sex. She tied his hands to the window above their bed-and lopped it off.

> July 2004 – A fifty year old German woman severs the penis of her 37-year-old Ghanaian ex-husband. He takes the knife from her and stabs her, ending her life. The man's organ was later found in the same room as her body.

> January 2002 – Pavel Morozov, an amputee, refuses to have sex with Olga Fedotov. She begins hitting him at this rejection of her offering. When he falls unconscious, she pulls down his pants and cuts off his penis. Then she stabs him in the chest. He dies and she is arrested for murder. She is sentenced to half the normal sentence for murder.

> July 1997 – Kim Phuong Tran severs her husband's penis while he is asleep. He had told her that he is in love with another woman. She is sentenced to two years house arrest, with community service. Part of her sentence was to take classes that promoted her understanding of the English language. She cut off his dick because of a language deficiency? Was something lost in the translation? Een amereeka we no cuttee off dickee, ok, mamasan? Men's rights groups in

Canada protested her light sentence.
> October 1997 – Nothing tops this one. An unnamed Thai wife cuts off the penis of her husband while he is asleep. She then ties it to helium balloons. Up, up, and away! Urban legend? Or just another case of penis envy taken to the extreme.
> March 1996- Tran Nhu Tran attempts to severe her husband's penis with a pair of scissors. She did not completely severe the penis. She was charged with "malicious wounding". The charges were later dropped.
> September 1992 – Sharmin Begum and her lovely sisters cut off the penis of Sharmin's husband, Abdul Motaleb, with a razor blade. At knifepoint he is forced to hold up his severed penis while the sisters laugh. It was in retaliation for wanting a divorce from Sharmin.

It is enough to make the average male afraid to go to sleep at night. Not only are women attacking the penis in record numbers- nothing is happening to them as a result. It becomes the butt of late night television jokes each time a man is horribly mutilated by his wife, or girlfriend. Each night a man that truly prizes his penis should pray to Priapus, the God of Erections. Here is a prayer that has been circulating office emails for years.

Now I lay me down to sleep,
I pray my penis I will keep.
And if I wake and it is gone,
I hope to find it on my lawn.
I hope the dog that is running free,
Does not find that part of me.
A small precaution I must take,
to keep this part I love to shake.

Much attention I must pay,
to ensure I put that knife away.
The mower, chainsaw, hatchet, too,
There's just no telling what she'll do,
To relieve me of my manly charm.
I must keep it safe from harm.
I cross my fingers as I close my eyes,
And also my legs to avoid surprise.
And if my penis takes a whack,
I pray the doctor can sew it back.

Ω

This wave of penectomies is not without historical precedent. The penis of Napoleon was reportedly severed at his autopsy. Urban legend reports that it was sold to a urologist for $40,000. That's the long and short of it, for the little Emperor. It was also alleged that Rasputin, the mad monk, had his member removed during the assassination that ended his existence on December 16, 1916. The legend says that is penis was saved and kept in a wooden box by his daughter, Maria. Freud would have a great time with this one! She kept it with her for many years. It was last reported to have been sold to the Russian government.

Look to see this one on EBay. A famous case from the 1930's is that of Kichizo Ishida. His lover, Sade Abe, strangled him during a hot sexual encounter. He dies in her hands (and in her!)Seeing her big chance she cuts off his penis. She carried it with her for days before surrendering it, and herself, to police. She served less than three years in jail and was granted amnesty in 1940. The last sighting of his penis was in a department store showcase in 1949. There was a movie made about the incident called In the Realm of the Senses. See if you can find it in your local video store.

Leveling the playing field by cutting off a man's most prized possession is the ultimate revenge of the penile envious. These are extreme examples. There is also the case of the 17-year-old girl from Harrisburg, Pennsylvania, that super glued her boyfriend's erect penis to his stomach to punish him for screwing around on her with another girl. He required medical attention, she was not charged.

The abuse of young males begins in our public school system. the abuse continues well into adulthood – to the point that men just accept and try to deal with the consistency of this society-approved violence as best as they can. Our fine young men are forced into a female dominated school system to get the priming for future attacks. Men benefit very little from marriage. After years of suffering the male has to endure the ultimate humiliation as his wife leaves him for another man. This is condoned by society and the woman is rewarded with the man's house, his children, his dignity, and most of his money. If the man tries to stand up for himself he will be sent to prison in accordance with laws that favor women. And some men experience a fate worse than death at the hands of their female companion-removal of the penis. All of this abuse starts in kindergarten for young American men-and never ends.

But what is the basis of this envy and disdain for the male appendage? Let's take a look at penis envy and its effect on the female disposition. But first, another brew.

8

PENIS ENVY

Appetizer
Moonshine

Main Course
Coors Banquet

Here is a fact of life. Women do not possess a penis. They were born without one. In the womb all human embryos begin as females. Then something unique and exclusive happens in about half of viable human embryos. A miraculous transformation occurs and they are converted into males. This is done through a series of changes that involve X and Y chromosomes. Remember your 10th grade Biology teacher? You should have listened up more. The personality of a female is focused on this omitted appendage. She is constantly searching for something she will never possess. This may the smoking gun as to why woman can never truly be happy with themselves.

At conception, the sperm donates either an X or a Y chromosome. These come from the father. The mother donates only X chromosomes. Once again the major decisions are left up to the male. For the first six weeks all embryos are female, possessing no sex differences, physical, hormonal, or structural. After six weeks the more intricate embryos break off from the norm and become males. Through the action of a gene on the Y chromosome called SRY (for "sex-determining region of the Y") male hormones are produced. These hormones inspire male reproductive organs and glands to rise above and differentiate from the existing female structures. Like Michelangelo crafting a masterpiece, the organs are sculpted by the phenomenally precise invisible chisel of nature. These hormones continue to advance the physical and intellectual development of the male until birth and beyond. The male hormones are responsible for the human males desire to explore, to create, to build, to philosophize , to mate, to wage peace, and to live a full life.

If the embryo is female, nothing spectacular happens and the indifferent structures of the female organs and glands continue to grow. It would be mathematically correct to state that men have exactly double the emotional, and intellectual, complexity as women. Men begin life as women and are astonishingly transformed into men. A male human being can "get in touch" with his feminine side from time to time if he needs to. Deciding which color to paint the kitchen, or which floral arrangement to send to their Aunt Edna's funeral are decisions gleaned from a man's residual feminine side. Women do not have this option. Women were conceived as women, developed as women, and remain women for their entire life. No transformation, no differentiation, no change, no duality of emotional and intellectual thought. The multifaceted conditioning that young male fetuses undergo simply does not occur with female embryos. Female human beings are distinctly one-dimensional. They cannot call upon their masculine side because they never had one. Although real men usually do not admit it, they can understand a woman's thought process quite well. The mistake that most men make is wishing that women could think more like men. Simply stated - while men can relate to a woman, women cannot relate to men. This is the cause of much dismay in relationships. The man that understands that women will never be capable of the deep thought (both emotional and intellectual) progression that men possess will understand why women are so difficult to understand (that last sentence will totally baffle a female human being).

Young female babies think differently than young male babies. The difference in infancy is noticeable only in general traits. Boys tend to explore more, girls tend not to. Boys move more, girls lay still. Minor differences. And then one day it happens. A young girl sees a penis. And she realizes that she does not have one. She has been slighted. The limited female internal thought process begins. Simple, basal, antediluvian, archaic thoughts. Originating in the same part of the female brain that triggers the rudimentary feeling of hunger. The nagging idea that the young female has been slighted somehow. Why does he have one and not me? Is there something wrong with me? Did I miss something? How can I get one? It is with these primitive thoughts originating from the hippocampus of the basal brain that female personalities begin to take shape. From infancy female human beings want something. They spend the rest of their life buying, borrowing and obtaining "stuff". By the time a female human being is in her twenties she has long forgotten the root of her feelings of want. She cannot remember past the gray cloud of seeing her first penis and realizing she had been shortchanged by nature. The yearning to quench the thirst of dehydrated emptiness had already formed her personality. Shopping gives a short feeling of well-being that soon wears off. So more shopping is then in order. It is an addiction. Something to stave off the buried desire of wanting a penis of their own. Women buy clothes that they never wear, only to encounter the vacancy in their mind again. The personality of a female human being is shaped by penis envy. It gives women a feeling of emptiness, of longing.

Men do not relate to this exclusively female experience. A man's emptiness only originates from a lack of production on the man's part. The man blames no one but himself for this feeling. And it can be rectified when he gets off his duff and starts producing what he wants.

Women do not possess this fine quality. They feel empty from childhood. It is a seed that has been planted in the young mind of the female and cultivated into adulthood. Many relationships have ended because of a women's inability to still the quaking preoccupations of their inner child's penis envy. A psychologist named Sigmund Freud became a household name by hitting close to the truth with his theories on woman and penis envy.

Sigmund Freud was born in Moravia, part of the Austrian Empire in 1856. Freud was an Austrian psychiatrist, and is credited with being the founder of psychoanalysis. Freud lived most of his life in Vienna, receiving his medical degree from the University of Vienna in 1881. Most woman psychologists discount Freud because of his insightful theories on sexual identity, repression, and penis envy. Freud thought that penis envy in girls had a very significant impact upon her sexual gender identity. Freud hypothesized that this discovery was a defining moment in the development of the female mindset. According to Freud, repression is a causative factor in the formation of the subconscious. Freud theorized that people may experience thoughts that are so distressing they cannot bear thinking consciously about these thoughts. The attempt is made to forget these thoughts. These thoughts are usually based on actual events. They try to banish these thoughts from their mind. These thoughts, feelings, and memories could not be banished from the mind altogether, but they could be banished from consciousness. They rest like sleeping dogs in the unconscious. People alter their lifestyles, their desires, and their actions in order to let these sleeping dogs lie. Freud observed that the process of repression is itself a non-conscious act. The young girl does not remember her mother saying sex was "bad" or "dirty"; she picks up on the uncomfortable cues that her mother sends her when there is a sexual feeling in the room. The sexual feeling could be a nude painting in a museum, or two dogs humping out in the backyard. The unconscious feeling that was fostered came from the child's desire to be accepted by the mother. In order to be accepted by her mother, the young girl accepted the mother's view that sex was "wrong". The basic desire for physical safety and emotional security overrode the young girl's natural urges and innate curiosity. As girls develop into woman the mother plays a crucial role in their attitudes on sex. (More on that in a later chapter.) Freud hypothesized that what people repressed was determined by their unconscious feelings. These feelings were subtle cues that had been picked up throughout life. In short, Freud proposed that the unconscious was both a cause and effect of repression. These powerful feelings were the result of three stages that were natural to human beings, the oral stage, the anal stage, and the phallic stage.

The "oral stage" comes from the pleasure a baby feels when it nurses (yum, yum) and fills its belly with mother's milk. This is followed by the tot's pleasure at emptying his/her bowels. Freud labeled this the "anal stage". These two powerful feelings are suppressed by the parents as the child grows older. This parental suppression leads to the individual "repression" of these strong drives. The drives never leave; they are just buried in the subconscious. Depending upon the individual, the repression of these drives may not be complete. They may manifest themselves in other behaviors that mimic the feeling without actually performing the action. Smoking a cigarette may be a substitute for the child that never got over missing his mommy's tit. Overeaters are described as being stuck in the "oral stage". Getting pleasure from anal sex, or other anal delights, may be the substitute for the repressed feeling of guilt the youth felt when he was scolded for shitting his pants. One could theorize that male homosexuals are stuck in the anal stage. (You may even find one that is on stage getting stuck in the anus!) Regardless of the causes of anal excitation, there are very few that can argue that taking a good shit is very satisfying, both physically and mentally. Mentally? Some may not believe that taking a shit is a mental relief. Then why the big smile when the deed is done? But let's move on past the anal stage. Both males and females will experience the oral and the anal stage according to Freud. The experiences that each endures will form parts of their personality that could take years for a therapist to unravel. The 'the phallic stage" is the preoccupation with the penis. It is experienced by both men and women. However, in very different ways.

Freudian theory has been called 'phallocentric' by some researchers. They think that Freud was preoccupied with the penis. Maybe so. Freud was human. Humans are preoccupied with the penis. It starts out as a toddler. When a young man first sees this magnificent appendage he is overjoyed. What a cool toy. But he soon realizes that this remarkable wand of pleasure is not necessary for survival. Its purpose is not clear. He begins to think someone is going to take it. And why not? They take all the other toys he is not supposed to have. This may be the root of the male fear of castration. Someone is going to take their favorite toy. It becomes an unconscious thought because it is too scary to think about. Most young men lock this phobia in their mental vault before they reach puberty. Young girls desire to have a penis. Especially if they have ever seen one. This is a desire that cannot be fulfilled. The empty, aching want gets locked in the mental vault of the female unconscious before the female reaches puberty. Boys have a phobic fear of castration lingering in their subconscious minds. Girls have a burning desire to possess a penis in theirs. Freud describes desire as a negative feeling; it is a lack of something. You desire what you don't have. You desire what you know that which you will never possess. And the repression of this desire is in direct proportion to the chances that you will fulfill this desire. The less of a chance of fulfilling a burning desire- the more you will re-press it. Freud made himself famous by teaching his patients to cope with subconscious desires.

This preoccupation with the male genitalia was the basis of females wanting a bigger penis in men. In other words, *If you have something that I do not have, I will act like I do not want it. I will pretend that it is not good enough for me. If I can make you feel as inadequate as I do, I will feel better.* This is very close to the way most woman treat the men in their lives. They are such penis addicts that they act like they could care less about their partner's penis. This deep- rooted envy interferes in their relationships with men. This idea has been the subject of many a discussion. The inevitable outcome of this discussion is to cause men to feel that their penis is not enough for their partners. Throughout history women have been responsible for each culture's obsession with the male appendage. One could go on to say that penis envy is the root cause of the penis size debate.

And some female human beings become too envious. They actually foster a disdain for the male species in order to compensate for their lack of a penis. They go overboard the other way. Making fun of men, picking apart every penile idiosyncrasy that men possess. Then they tell their girlfriends. Yes, partner, all of her friends know the innermost details of the structure of your cock. Your privates become public as soon as you stick them in one female. Fueled by penis envy, she feels the need to disparage your cock to all of her friends, even if it is subtle. That is why they are looking at you with knowing smiles. They know. They know because your loving sex partner told them. Hey, if she can't have one, why treat any of them with respect? Most men do not mind the jabs; some even perpetuate the verbal assaults and pecker assassinations in order to make women feel better about themselves. Consider the following exchange between two bank tellers from Charlotte, North Carolina.

"How is it going with your new boyfriend?"
"Great. We are really hitting it off."
"Oh, that means you are screwing him!"
"Stop, you are so nasty! So what if I am."
"I knew it. Well, is he hung?"
"Stop. You are embarrassing me."
"C'mon, let me in on it. Is he hung?"
"Not really. But that doesn't matter to me."
"Yeah, right. Me either."
"It kind of curves to the left. Is that normal?"
"Kind of. I screwed this guy once that was curved to the right. You remember Troy? He was a 'rightie' if I ever had one."
"Did I ever tell you about Greg? Oh... my... God. He had the biggest ...."

Well you know the rest of the story. Men do not care about the size of their penises. They are concerned because women care about size. Women have been preoccupied with penis size throughout recorded history. There is a long history of men attempting to satisfy a woman's disappointment of their genital size by enlarging their penis. Evidence of penis enlargement attempts can be found from ruins thousands of years ago. From paintings and drawings it is believed that men hung stones from their penis around 4000 years ago. There is even some suggestion that the Pharaohs of ancient Egypt used the hanging method to be better hung. Perhaps the root of the word "hung" is derived from this ancient practice. It is still in even casual conversations today.

Let us not think for a minute that men hung stones and painfully stretched their pricks for any other reason than to impress women. This method is currently being practiced in modern day Africa. The Caramoja tribe of northern Uganda still try to make their schlongs longer by tying a round stone disk to the top of their manhood. As they get used to the pain, more stones are added. Evidence of this stone hanging practice has been found worldwide. The Cholomecs, an extinct tribe form ancient Peru, would suspend increasingly heavy weights on their peckers, starting with boys as young as five years old. We barely send our boys to kindergarten at this age, never mind suspend stones from their dicks. The Kama Sutra, the acrobatic bible for the sexually adventurous, mentions the practice of stone hanging. The Sadhus of northern India believe that the spirit of God resides in the penis of every man. They start hanging small weights from preadolescent boys in order to reach a spiritual connection with the God of the Penis. The weights do not get removed. Sometimes these "ancient" cultures stumble on to something that makes sense to modern medical science. Starting the stone stretching practice on young males is more effective. The formative ligament hasn't fully developed and stretches more readily in young males than males past the age of puberty. Over many years the penis may stretch from one to three feet long. Most of their wangs are useless-it is just a thin piece of stretched tissue. If the stones are not hung properly the cells of the penis may die. This necrosis of the tissue will cause the penis to die and eventually slough off. The practices of the Sadhus was made into a film called Dances Sacred and Profane. In this video you will see the weights hanging from the penises of young boys. All of this for the visual appeal of the female of the species. In every society throughout history there exist references to the penis.

The Japanese celebrate by walking in parades with large phalluses in front of them. The main reason is to quell the complaints of the women that were complaining about the size of their men's organs. Even today the internet is full with magical stretching devices that claim to enlarge the penis. Men, in their attempt to please women, buy this shit in lots. The women sit back and allow the men to justify their penises to them. Penis envy is driving the penis size controversy. Sometime the wife is referred to as the "old ball and chain". That could be a reference to the various devices men would attach to their penis in order to make it longer for his wife. It is penis envy that first inspired women to complain against the size of their man's penis. Our history is full of artwork, sculpture, poetry, paintings, and literary references to the size of a man's penis. In order to impress the picky female onlookers, men have resorted to various mutilating techniques. All in the name of catching the admiring glance of a receptive female. Penile mutilation is present on all continents in all cultures.

Contemporary men have even tried surgery in modern times to have a larger penis that would satisfy women. The surgery, known as the Bihari Procedure, may have its origins in ancient China. The modern technique is actually named after an Egyptian doctor, Dr. J. Bihari. Dr. Bihari was one of the first doctors to try this procedure in the early 1990's. The procedure will make you want to hold your crotch in fear. There is a ligament that suspends the penis during erection. You can even flex this ligament. The next time you get a hard on, stand in front of a mirror. You might want to first make sure that you are alone in the house. With your hands on your hips let your member sag a little. It will naturally droop. When it gets to half mast-snap it to attention. (It may take some practice.)You may even want to yell, in military fashion, "Attention!" to stimulate the little guy to stand up. Have some fun with it. Turn sideways and really watch the range of motion that you have. Put a nickel on the head of your penis and see how far you can "flick" it. Start a contest. The Pecker Nickel Flicking Contest. Not for the faint of heart. Anyway, this action is caused by the suspensory ligament. This ligament is responsible for holding the penis up when it gets hard.

During the Bihari Procedure, this ligament is severed. This allows the penis to hang down more because of gravity. It actually hangs like a condemned man on the gallows. The man's stretched broken neck is analogous to the suspensory ligament. Your man will never stand at attention again. He is defeated, dejected, pointing downward. He is also pointing down with an extra 1.5 inches. You paralyze your best friend; just so some slut can see you hang down another inch and a half. Better have another slug.

But that is not the worst of it. Some men will not gain any length from this procedure. Some experience a condition called fibrosis. This is a shrinking and toughening of the sensitive cells of the penis. In other words – it shrinks as a reaction to the cutting. So now the hapless man has a shorter, but tougher, penis. I cannot speak for everyone- but I do not want a "tough" penis. I will fight all his fights for him. He need not be a tough guy. He just needs to be there for me-to be ready to go when I am ready to go. In addition, another side effect of the surgery is permanent impotence. Shorter, tougher, and limp. I don't even like my steaks that way, never mind my cock. All of this to satisfy the female need to ridicule the penis out of a repressed desire to own one of their own.

Men have been at it for centuries. There are many options in the penis enhancement surgery manual. You can have a doctor inject fat from your gut, or your fat ass, into your dick. You are just redistributing the wealth. This could add from 30% to 50% in girth. Women love girth. But there are problems. You can lose weight. And guess which pile of fat goes first? Nature is a cruel mistress. Your little operation deflates when you get on Jenny Craig. It seems ironic. You get on Jenny Craig so you can lose weight to be more sexually attractive to your wife. You have a fat ass and a fat dick. But they are not mutually exclusive. If you lose one, you lose the other. If only you had a wife that liked fat guys. Then you could have this surgery.   Also, the implanted fat can redistribute itself.. Kind of like putting Jell-o into a sandwich bag and squeezing. The shit moves all over the goddamn place. You are having sex with your wife, she squeezes her pussy, and all of the fat squishes down around the base of the shaft. You look like you have a beer bottle for a pecker. Not good. And definitely not sexy. Unless you get a "Budweiser" logo tattooed on it. You could then appeal to the beer drinking set of women. Men go to extravagant lengths to show their lengths.

In her book "Are Men Necessary?" author Maureen Dowd epitomizes the Freudian theory of repressed penis envy. The references to the Y chromosome as being redundant and vestigial are classic penis envy feelings. Ms. Dowd does not, nor will she ever, possess a Y chromosome. We make fun of that which we desire most. Dowd uses the Y chromosome as a penile euphemism. Her envy for the male appendage is pathetically classic. But she has managed to hide her simmering penis envy under an intellectual front. It's a great book, but the themes of penis envy and jealously of the intellect of the human male taint the otherwise insightful book. To answer the question posed in the title of Ms. Dowd's book – no, men are not necessary. Neither is food. Or love. None of these are necessary. Except that a woman would cease to exist if it were not for all three.

Okay, woman could exist without men. What kind of an existence would woman have without men? Well, let's first take away all of the buildings (will women develop building envy?). It was man that introduced architecture into human culture. Women do not possess the brain structure to manipulate three dimensional objects in their mind. This quality is necessary for the visual spatialization men use to build objects in their mind before putting them on paper, and ultimately into reality. There would be no technology, television, radio, cell phones, CD players, lights, etc. - all products that were invented by men. To keep it brief, woman would be naked, with overgrown pubic areas, in the wild, starving to death (or eating berries). The main loss that woman would feel if there were no men would be emotional. With no men on the planet, women would have nothing to talk about. Penis envy has deep reaching psychological roots that grow entwined into a society that is becoming increasingly hostile toward the possessor of the penis.

Freudian theory of penis envy was enriched by Carl Jung. Jung introduced the Electra complex as the female counterpart to the male Oedipus complex. Oedipus, a tragic figure, journeyed through life only to end up sleeping with his mother. The Oedipus complex was detailed by Freud as a powerful repressed sexual feeling that young men feel towards their mothers as they reach puberty. That's pee shivers gross if you think about it too long.

Stop thinking about it. Drink up.

The Electra complex comes from the Greek myth of Electra, a saucy bitch who wanted her brother to avenge their father Agamemnon's death by killing their mother Clytemnestra. Jung used this to explain the friction between young girls and their mothers. According to this theory, young girls are very emotionally attached to their mothers. From birth. One sad day the little girl discovers she has no penis. The infinite ways this could happen would fill all of the books ever printed and still not cover each situation fully. When she discovers that she lacks a penis during the phallic_stage the daughter becomes sexually attracted to her father. But it is more that she thinks he will give her a penis. Up until this stage she has gone to him for everything. He usually gives in. Deep in her subconscious mind she really wants a penis. Dad seems like the most likely candidate to give her one (I mean does he even use it?). She feels that Mom, who gave birth to her, left her deficient. She becomes more hostile towards her mother. It is her mother's fault that she was not born with the penis that her brothers, dad, and all the other males possess.

As stated in a previous chapter, her brain is different. Studies on the brain show that females are psychologically subordinate to men. Both intellectually and emotionally. It is not only wired differently, but the female brain has different reactions to the same stimuli. Different emotions are stored into different parts of the subconscious. Penis envy is exclusively a female problem. Therefore the female brain must be able to process this problem and make sense of it. Or conceal it deep with the confines of the subconscious. Keep anyone from ever looking at it. Indiana Jones, that finder of lost treasures, would not be able to penetrate the Labyrinth of the Deceptive Female Mind, riddled with traps and diversions, to capture the truth. Females center their behavior towards men based on their multifaceted resentment of having been shortchanged at birth. The male brain does not have to deal with this problem at all. Men have penises. No envy necessary. This may be contributing to the belief that females have a weaker ego. The part of the personality where morality is developed and values internalized is compromised in females by the invasive tendrils of penis envy. It is the basis of rationalizing behavior. A poor person can rationalize stealing an apple from a cart. This is easy. Consider the thought pattern of the homeless street urchin as he considers stealing an apple.

I am hungry. Starving. There are dozens of apples on that cart. The rich cart owner will not miss one apple. He has dozens of apples. Some apples are going to go bad. Yeah, that's right; this apple is probably going to go bad. That's why I am taking it. Damn rich people, they charge too much for apples anyway. They are the real thieves! I deserve to eat. God did not mean for me to starve while some people throw apples away. I am taking an apple.

This rationalizing behavior allows us to do things that we know we should not. Rationalizations can be as simple as sneaking candy into a movie theater. *(Hey, I ain't paying $5.00 for a bag of popcorn!)* Or it could be as complex as a lifelong disdain and loathing of men because they have something you do not. A disdain and loathing whose cause has been hidden. Hidden from the person that buried the feelings in the first place. The subconscious is a tricky maze. The pathway to self-knowledge is hidden to us by ourselves. It is the keeper of the secret that knows the secret. The keeper is hiding the secret from himself. That takes a lot of tricky psychological moves. These moves translate into behavior directed at other human beings. In a phallocentric society the young girl learns to survive by acceding to men. She learns to flourish by manipulating men. The irony is that she manipulates men using the penis that she so secretly desires to possess. The man's penis. It is not long before she realizes that he can be led by his penis. She can use his sex drive against him. Do you think I am joking? This behavior carries into their sex lives also. The subconscious longing to have her own penis is evidence in her cries of passion. How many times have you heard a women, in the throes of orgasm, yell,

"Fill me, oh yes, I want it all." Or *"Give it to me, yes give it to me!"*

Some men would think that they mean good loving. Or that the female wants his member real bad. Well, guess what boys; she does want your dick very bad. Except not the way you think. She wants it off of you and attached to her - thirty years ago! So the next time she says,

"I want it!" or *"I really want you to give it to me tonight!"* be careful.

You may think that the meaning is deeply ingrained in an unhappy person's desire to own and use to its full capacity an organ that they will never be able to own or possess without your consent. That is why women's personalities are so difficult to understand. It is like Marie Antoinette, French aristocrat, wealthy beyond anyone's dreams. Marie could not understand the plight of the poor since she had never been poor. When she was told that the poor had no bread to eat she quipped, "Let them eat cake!" This is how men see women when it comes to penis envy. They do not understand the deep impact of being born without a wang, the psychological feeling of loss, or of being slighted. And they try to please their women in other ways. Looking for the "piece of cake" that will feed the psychologically starving female in their lives.

The young man who perpetually complains to his buddies that he cannot do anything to please his wife is correct. Upon reading this chapter the now-enlightened young man will realize he was right; he cannot make his wife happy. Among other deficiencies and disorders, his wife, like most woman, suffer from a deep psychological craving that they do not even understand. They just know that they need something that they do not possess and the man has it. So they continue to take and consume everything the man in their life has to give them. Male human beings that attempt to satisfy this need soon find themselves emotionally and physically exhausted. But alas, young man, you cannot go back twenty or thirty years in time and attach a penis to your wife so she could grow up with one. (Stop thinking about it.) In order to carry on you need to realize that penis envy has shaped the personality of your loving, significant other. You must comprehend that it is the sad fate of female human beings to always want to fill this need, or need to fill this want. Women will languish trying to solve this biological enigma; usually by running their man into the ground as he tries to get her to answer the enduring question that has plagued mankind for centuries.

"What is wrong, honey?"

9

PARENTAL INFLUENCE

Appetizer
One shot of Chambord

Main Course
Miller Genuine Draft

Your ex-wife obtained her views on marriage and sex from her mother. Her mother was the main influence on her life from birth until the last time she called to reinforce her teachings. Left over from the "Age of Repression" is the mindset that good girls do not like sex - they tolerate it. The Sexual Revolution of the sixties and seventies has freed some females from the grip of this invisible repressor. But the notion that a married woman is not sexually *with her husband* being still pervades our life as we tiptoe into the twenty-first century. It is very possible that your ex-wife ruined your marriage by the subtle signals sent to her by her mother.

The old joke goes:

"How do you turn a girl off on sex?"

"You marry her!"

That's a real funny joke-unless you are married and then the joke is on you. Do your shot. Make it a double. This chapter is brutal.

Ω

Here we are in the 21st century. You must know a couple that has been married for at least ten years. Approach them with the question, "How is your sex life?" You may get varying answers, but a scientific study would reveal that the husband feels less affection from his wife than he did in previous years. He feels rejected and neglected by this once warm and sexual being. Maybe the relationship just cooled down, I mean with soccer practice and running a house- who has time for sex? Or maybe, just maybe, it is far more sinister than that. Maybe your sex life has an uninvited visi- tor; your mother-in-law. Her mother has slowly put out the fires of your raging sex life. Sure, the kids and daily life has put a damper on it. She can no longer meet you at the door dressed in saran wrap when you come home from a hard day at the office. She now greets you wrestling with a screaming baby with a drooping diaper full of amazing hues of green and brown. That's part of life and you have come to accept it. Beyond the workings of raising a family, there is another unseen force affecting your passion. It is the voice of her mother (and grandmother, and great- grandmother, etc, etc, etc.) that is putting the burning fire of desire totally out. It is not quite as overt as a bucket of ice water poured on your crotch as you lay in bed. But it is just as effective.

Her method of sexual deletion is more like a computer virus. When you were first married the virus lay dormant. Living in an apartment did not set it off. So you humped just about everywhere like puppies on an oyster diet. But then the inevitable buying of the house and filling it with kids came along. The house that she selected. You know that you convinced yourself that it was mutual decision. But it was her choice. If it was totally your choice you would have bought a log cabin with a wagon-wheel coffee table and moose head on the wall. (Did you notice how much time the real estate agent spent talking to your wife? You were just along for the ride, buddy!) Paying for it was another of your duties. Things changed, didn't they? Once in the house the virus was activated. Your stuff disappeared. Your remote-controlled airplanes did not exist anymore. Your poster of Michael Jordan was nowhere to be found. Something like this:

The Man: "Honey did you see my barbells? They were in the spare room."
The Woman: "What?" (she heard every word clearly).
The Man: "My barbells." (walks upstairs to the bath room where his wife is on the toilet) "They were in the spare room, I work out with them…"
The Woman: "Oh, those rusty things? I put them in the garage. They were in the way. Besides, I want to setup that room for the baby."
The Man: "Baby? We're having a baby!"
The Woman: "Well, not right away."
The Man: "But I thought we agreed to wait until next year. Are you…?"
The Woman: "No, I am not pregnant. But I will be - eventually. And I want to start cleaning the place up. We don't need those nasty barbells denting up the new rug anyway."
The man: (still reeling from the "baby" remark) Oh, well, I guess…"
The Woman: "Also, can you do something with that coffee table? I really don't think a fish tank coffee table is what we need in the living room."
The man: "But I have had that for years. The guys love it! Where are we going to put our beer and our pretzels when we watch the football game?"
The Woman: "And that's another thing…"

Slow, methodical, one way, and permanent. Your bachelor ways were absorbed by your wife and marked for deletion. The new house you were paying for was decorated by two people. Your ex-wife and her mother. The virus was slowly working your single bachelor possessions into one big file marked " OBSOLETE". Stored in the garage and ultimately removed. Some things you watched disappear. Like all of your single friends. Other things, like the whereabouts of your red and green Christmas socks, will remain a mystery. Etched into your ex-wife's subconscious was a clear route the "virus" was to follow. Remove all of the vestiges of your single life, eradicate any history of your former self was her goal. The virus strengthened along the way, justifying its' past behavior and solidifying future plans. The virus was a copy, with minor variations, of the one that her mother's mother had implanted in her. And her mother's mother's mother's mother's mother. That brings us back to the early 1800's. Then we can apply the same mother's mother sequential chronology until we find that we are in the time of the Dark Ages. This is where the "virus" of repression was first allowed to spread.

Tempered by time, adjusted by society, the "virus" has been in place since the first repressor worked its deeds upon his expressive wife. Free-spirited women, dancing nude in the woods were labeled as witches. The "church" was on a mission to rid the world of free-thinking sexual women. The real goal of the Spanish Inquisition, Salem Witch trials, and other pursuits of the church was to rid society of Cave Harlot forever (remember Cave Harlot?). And they were not gotten rid of easily. At the heart of all women lies the vestigial behavior alleles of Cave Harlot. During the Dark Ages, assertive women were beaten, tortured, and/or burned at the stake in an attempt to curb the unfettered sexuality of women. Your ex-wife is the result of centuries of artificial selection. The openly-sexual females were all but removed from the gene pool, thanks to the oppressive actions of the Christian "church". Horny women everywhere were taught to repress, or at least hide, their sexual proclivities. This repression has been passed down from mother to daughter as a means of survival in a brutal "religious" world. The Muslims also dealt harshly with Cave Harlot.

Muslim women, to this day, are put to death for following their innate biological breeding strategy. Sexual repression has been artificially selected for just like breeding poodles from wolves. What was once a mighty beast has been reduced to a controllable coward that we can dress up the way we want. But at the heart of the prissy poodle lies the venerable she-wolf. If let loose into the wild the feral poodle would revert back to its natural state within a few generations. The dormant genes that have been selected against would rise to the surface and dominate the unnatural genes for poufy white hair and pranciness. The same is true of the genes for Cave Harlot.

As a result of this selective breeding (is there a pun there?) your mother-in-law excluded sexual exploration from your marriage long before she ever met you. She worked hard every day for over twenty years to teach your future ex-wife to reduce your penis to a "hands-on" condition. (Unless your ex-wife is one of the surviving descendents of "Cave Harlot." In that case I have one thing to say to you. Go to the next chapter you lucky bastard- this does not apply to you.) But if your ex-wife is one of the countless millions that have allowed her mother's sexual mores to run your life then I implore you to read on (and wallow in self-pity). You thought getting married would be a non-stop exploration of each other's bodies? Garter belts, lingerie, shaving her pussy, maybe even a 'ménage a trois' with one of her cute friends. You dreamed of her wearing high heels with a short miniskirt and nothing underneath. You dreamed of her walking up to you, dressed for an evening of dancing, in a sultry voice, whispering in your ear:

"I'm not wearing any panties."

And then flashing you as you returned from the rest room, only to prompt a quick trip to the car to make the beast with two backs while the windows steamed up.

Boy, were you wrong! While some women may do these "things" at first, the mother-in-law virus soon takes over. Sex every night in every room in the house turns into sex every other night, and then only in the bedroom. And then maybe once a week. The garter belts are put away to make way for control top panty hose (with reinforced cotton crotch). Her mother goes with her to buy them. Four pair, at least. That's why it is so important for her to go shopping with her mother. This isn't a relaxed mother-daughter bonding event. This is the genealogical extermination of all things sexual. Her mother points to the big cotton briefs with reinforced crotch and says:

"Those look nice".

Your ex-wife bought two pair. She wore them to bed nightly. Ugh! The long, flowing hair that would lightly tickle your sack while receiving oral sex was nice. One day her mother took her to the hair salon (this is usually after the birth of the second child). And then your ex-wife came home with short hair. Your nut sack wrinkled in disgust. No more light tickles, boys. No more oral sex, either. She may blame the haircut on the baby (she pulls it all the time!). She used to beg you to yank it while plowing her doggy style. But those days are over. The once-a-week sexual encounter becomes routine. No dirty talk, no fantasy, no… future? You see, while you were dreaming of exploring wild sex with your ex-wife, your mother-in-law had different plans for your marriage. She had plans of you providing her daughter with a house, a couple of kids, and a "nice" vacation every year. She had plans that did not include you reawakening any dormant vestigial gene of "Cave Harlot" that may have been passed down undetected over the generations. Her mother before her, and her mother before that, had worked hard to eliminate sexual activity from their married life. The church demanded no less. It had become pure survival during the Dark Ages to repress female sexuality. Only good girls survived the pyres of

Christianity. So they all became good girls. And good girls did not consort with the devil. Good girls did not have active sexual lives with their husbands either. They "tolerated" his advances once in a while. Pulled up their nightgowns as necessary. They wanted to survive. The church had forced them to believe that sex was wrong, and the enjoyment of sex was a sin unless it was for having children. Your ex-wife is the descendent of the church-imposed elimination of sex from the civilized life-style. So as you lie awake in "Blue Ball Land", your ex-wife is sleeping soundly. She is providing a warm, nutritious place for the virus of a sex-less marriage to grow. She is doing what was taught to her by her mother.

Ω

You will get the benefit of watching her slowly turn into her mother. It is a slow process. A few pounds this year, a few pounds next year. Here a pound, there a pound, everywhere a pound-pound. Ol' MacDonald had a cow. Ee Yi Yee Yi ….boo hoo. At first, you tolerate it.

Maybe she does have a headache.

You make excuses for it.

Well, the kids are a handful.

You allow a thought to creep into your mind that maybe she is....*Naaa, it's just the kids, and the new house, and, well, she's tired all the time. Things will get better. I'll just immerse myself at work.*

Her mother watched the virus replicate. Her wishes became your nightmare. Her daughter grew more like her every day. Sort of like an evil scientist trying to take over the world she laughs to herself alone as she drives from your house.

"Wa hahaha. WA HAHAHA."

Another one bites the dust. Another man follows the

"virus" into a life sentence. She has taught her daughter well. Now she must make sure the granddaughters know. Yes, teach the children well...Meanwhile you are living the way the "virus" wants you to live.

Work hard so my kids can have nice stuff.

You get up early for work, and you don't even know why. You stay late. You come home and yell at the evening news just to redirect your anger and frustration.

Goddamned politicians, they're all crooks. Frigging multinational corporations...Aaaaggghh!

After dinner you think,

"Is this my third, or fourth, beer?"

As you drift off to sleep (in the recliner) you remember that you were once a man with dreams. A man that had time to go out with the guys, have a beer, check out the chicks, go fishing. As your eyes get heavy your fat, short-haired, cotton-brief-underwear-wearing wife is sleeping soundly in your bed. The "virus" implanted in her by her mother has replicated and infests every cell in her body. Instead of making the beast with two backs-she *looks* like the beast with two backs. In your sleep you shudder at the idea of going upstairs to be with her. Your dreams are haunted by a twisted, reversed version of the "Stepford Wives" in which all of the wives are becoming fat, short-haired versions of their mothers. You awake from sleep with a start. *Oh, God, no!!* You look around and realize that the nightmare is real. One more beer, and the Playboy Channel will kill the pain. Meanwhile across town your mother-in-law is smiling in her sleep. She awakes from a sound sleep, laughing...

"Wa hahaha. WA HAHAHA."

Ω

When your ex-wife and her mother talk they will exchange subtle messages to one another regarding the asexual lifestyle each of them is pursuing. The virus implanted in your ex-wife by her mother is multiplying steadily. And remember, any attempt to communicate how you feel will not be understood by the unrefined communication system that women still possess. You are on your own sexually. It's either your hand (and the internet), or you release the caveman that is buried inside your limbic brain and risk losing your wonderful "marriage".

Even the casual student of Greek mythology knows the story of Medusa. The common belief is that if one were to look at Medusa directly they would turn to stone. But the story of Medusa may be allegory for the institution of marriage. Medusa was one of the three Gorgon sisters. Everyone knew of the Gorgon sisters, they were pretty hot. They would make great wives. Medusa was originally very beautiful. She also had a day job as a priestess of Athena. Athena, or Pallas Athena, was one of the most powerful goddesses in Greek mythology. Athena was the daughter of Zeus. Not someone to screw around with. So Medusa is working for Athena, and she is very beautiful, some consider her even more beautiful than Athena. Athena doesn't like this very much but doesn't make a big stink. Now Athena also has a thing for Poseidon, God of the Sea. Poseidon had a reputation as a lady's man, having slept with a number of Greek tarts. But Athena is a virgin, and wants to remain so. Medusa knows this and uses her beauty to lure Poseidon to sample her wares. Cave Harlot emerges in Greek mythology. Anyway Medusa not only slept with Poseidon, but she slept with Poseidon in Athena's temple. Athena found out and turned Medusa into the snake-haired horror that turn men to stone if they even glance at her. The analogy here is obvious. Your ex-wife may have started off as a beauty, passionately screwing you in every room of the house. But given a few years you found it hard to even look at her for fear of turning to stone.

Ω

But her mother's influence does not stop in your bedroom. You should be so lucky. She took cues from her
mother her whole life. She was in constant Freudian conflict with needing acceptance from her mother and blaming
her for not giving birth to her with a penis. Your ex-wife
and her mother had a very special relationship. It was based
on tension. The mother also dealt with powerful repressed
feelings towards her daughter. The feelings she experienced
she should not feel as a mother, as prescribed by society.
These were in contrast to the feelings that she felt as a
woman. Yes, like it or not your mother –in – law was once
a sexual being. Yeah! Yuck. Just as the daughter was
reaching puberty and sprouting all the characteristic protu-
berances that define an adolescent, the mother was watching her hair turn gray and her ass sag. Mom felt torn between the maternal behaviors she should be exhibiting and
the threat she felt by her own daughter's budding sexuality.
This conflict of feelings is not handled well by the female
mind. Some mothers fill in these feelings with criticism.
They become overly critical of their daughter in an effort to
control her. Each day, the mom will criticize the child in a
subtle form of brainwashing that keeps the young lady from
developing her sexual self. Some of this stems from penis
envy. Remember from the previous chapter the complex
subconscious. The penis envy felt by the mother was transferred onto her own daughter. Mom was going to be replaced sexually. Mothers do not like to be replaced. Their
egos cannot handle the emotional strain. Avenues of pain
that have long been closed to traffic may open up. Constantly criticizing her daughter keeps her daughter in line.
From the time the child begins to take an interest in her hair
the mother is there to quell this sexual expansion. Consider
the case of Debbie C., a nurse at a major hospital in Cleve-
land, Ohio.

As a young girl I had a great relationship with my mother. She was a stay-at-home mom. My dad was a manager at a local restaurant. Mom and I would hang out alone a lot on weekends and holidays. Dad usually had to work on these days. When Dad was home, I was usually in school-or he was too tired to play with me. Anyway, I was real close to my mother. We did everything together. When I got my period, she withdrew from me. Nothing major, but I felt that I had done something, something wrong. She didn't hug me as much. She was very uncomfortable with the whole Kotex pad idea. I received minimal support from her during this confusing time. As the years went on I developed breasts. They were really nice. I wanted to share this joy with my mother but she withdrew from me even further every time I would try to broach the subject. I learned to confide in friends. I learned about the birds and the bees from my friend, Julie. I felt abandoned by my mother. I dressed for boys. I liked the attention. I still do. Around this time my mother criticized everything that I did. We had a lot of arguments about my clothes, the music I listened to, and the friends I hung out with. It was like she was trying to keep me as a child. I even said that to her during one of our arguments. Everything I did she criticized. She got pretty nasty at times. She would tell me to lose weight, or do something with my hair, or tell me I had my father's nose. I hated her. The feeling of tension between us exists to this day. She is constantly criticizing how I raise my children, my cooking on holidays; you know, just snippy remarks-but they still hurt. Whenever she is around there is tension. After she leaves, my husband and I usually argue. He can't stand her. I wish I could have kept the relationship with her that I had as a child. Last week I broke down into tears when my oldest daughter told me that I was always criticizing her. I guess history repeats itself. Oh, God. Oh, God.

This type of tension between a mother and daughter is not uncommon. The daughter feels rejected and abandoned by her mother just when she needs her most. The daughter takes her cues from her mother. As the young girl enters into her adult years she turns more to these cues. Marriage is a difficult state. Like you don't know that? There is no training that can prepare a person for this journey into the unknown. Girls become their mothers. This is the only thing that they know. In order to survive she regresses to the techniques and ideas that her mother taught her. The only template that she possesses was framed out by her mommy. And, since she knows no other way, she begins to apply this template to her own marriage. From the role of sex in her relationship with her husband to the relationship that she fosters with her own children, her mother is directing her behavior. Drink the rest of that beer and open another.

If your mother-in-law berated her husband, you will be berated. It is part of the female psyche to "badmouth" their men. This behavior could be charted as a range. The behavior exists, but it is subject to implementation. Females disdain males. That is accepted. It is the degree that the male feels this contempt that is important. Did your mother-in-law nag her husband every day? If so, guess what you are in for? There is no way to say that all females will behave in the same way. Everyone has individual differences due to perceptions, experiences, and the amount of their behavior that have chosen to change. But there are trends. Women have tendencies. It is not hard to image that a young girl will set up the same marital experiences for her husband that her mother setup for the girls' father. The influence of the mother is too great. The way the table is set comes from her mother. The time that you eat dinner comes from her mother. In the book, "Toxic Parents", Dr. Susan Forward gives us some insight into this complex behavior. Dr. Forward says that people reenact past conflicts in order to gain some control over them. If the child grew up with an alcoholic then she would most likely marry an alcoholic. It doesn't make sense that someone who knew the pain that alcoholism causes would jump right in to a relationship with anyone that even resembles an alcoholic. This behavior is incomprehensible to forward thinking humans. Dr. Forward gives us some insight into this complex, defeating behavior:

Adult children of alcoholics frequently marry alcoholics. Many people find it bewildering that someone who grew up in the chaos of an alcoholic family would choose to relive the trauma. But the drive to repeat familiar patterns of feelings is common to all people, no matter how painful or self-defeating those feelings may be. The familiar provides a sense of comfort and structure for our lives. We know what the rules are, and we know what to expect. More important, we reenact past conflicts because this time we hope to make it come out right-we're going to win the battle. This reenactment of old, painful experiences is called a "repetition compulsion."

I use the alcoholic as a basis to make a point. Everyone is familiar with at least one alcoholic family's plight. It is not hard to understand the concept of "repetition compulsion" when it is put into a familiar light. Men also repeat their childhood traumas. But women do so on an order of magnitude greater than men. Men learn to deal with them and put them to rest. Women bring their childhood conflicts into their marriage. What better place to reenact the feelings instilled in her by her mother than to marry a facsimile of her father? She may even be wrong. They marry a guy that is not at all like their father. They soon attribute everything that the poor sap does as the work of their father-and hold the husband accountable for them becoming their mother. Let's expand on this line of thinking.

The conflicts between a young girl and her mother cannot be solved by the young girl during her childhood. She is just a child. The conflicts stay in her subconscious until she becomes an adult. They remain there, dormant, viable, and ready to activate when the situation is correct. She is going to get these conflicts resolved. Period. The most common, and easiest, way she can do this is to recreate the situation. She must recreate her mother's marriage. From soup to nuts (euphemism for sex). Everything is recreated, with only minor variation. Then she can go back (in her mind only) and fight the oppressor, and the oppression, as an adult. On a level playing field. The oppressor is her mother. The oppression is her sexuality and rights as an individual. But she will not simply call her mother up one day and cuss her out. No sirree, Bob. That is too simple and direct for the female mind. She is going to recreate the circumstances and become everything that she disliked about her mother. Like Dr. Forward has said, she is doing this because it is comfortable and secure. It is comfortable and secure to repress her sexuality-she watched her mom do it for years. It is comfortable and secure to keep her husband's needs at bay. She watched her mom do it for years. As I have said before, these are a range of behaviors, a sliding scale if you will. Your ex-wife had nothing to do with her body developing into a female. It was how this was perceived by her mother that set the tone for your ex-wife's view on sex. It was her mother's daily behavior that set the tone for what you are experiencing now. You do marry the girl's mother. There is a real good chance that your ex-wife's mother did not physically abuse her after she became a teenager. The mother probably stopped hitting her as soon as she became able, and willing, to hit her mother back. From the teen years on, the mother beat your ex-wife down with verbal abuse. Remember the difference. With verbal abuse, the bruises are all on the inside.

Most people would opt to get a slap once a week than to be verbally abused daily. The slap hurts, there is no doubt about it. But you can get on with your life. When constantly berated, criticized, and demeaned, you tend to develop phobias, irrational behaviors and poor self-image. This verbal abuse is the main form of control exercised by women toward men. Sadly enough, it is also the main form of control directed at their children. Especially their daughters. The verbal abuse peaks during the adolescent years. Some case studies show that daughters report daily attacks upon their appearance, intellect, capability, and development as a human being. The powerful feelings of inadequacy created by verbal abuse manifest themselves in a variety of behaviors. The behaviors are as extreme as the verbal abuse. The bruises that they leave on the inside may never heal. And this abuse cycles from your mother-in-law to your ex-wife. And ultimately to you and your children.

Dario Maestripieri of the University of Chicago has been studying abusive relationships in one of our close primate relatives. Maestripieri's report appears in the July 5 Proceedings of the National Academy of Sciences. Maestripieri's team studied a large group of Rhesus monkeys at an outdoor facility in Georgia. The team had noticed there was physical abuse directed from the mother to her offspring. This was in contradiction to the notion that all primates show good maternal care. The group of researchers transferred some newborns to different, non-abusive mothers. Maestripieri found that abuse by the mother is a learned trait. According to Maestripieri, abusive rhesus monkey mothers regularly kick, hit, bite, and otherwise brutalize their babies. The offspring of these abusive females grow up to become abusive parents themselves. None of the females that were reared by non-abusive mothers became an abusive parent. Maestripieri believes that this is an example of perpetuating a primate cycle of family violence. Maestripieri believes that perpetuating abuse needs two factors. First is that the rhesus mothers that abused their children were abused by their mothers. This was true whether the mother was the biological, or adoptive, parent of the young monkey. The second factor is that females born to abusive mothers become non-abusive mothers if raised by an adoptive, non-abusive mother. "Rhesus monkeys are an excellent animal model of human child abuse," Maestripieri asserts. "The ways in which these behaviors are transmitted across generations in monkeys and people may be very similar," he adds.

We may not be monkeys, but we share similar heritage.

Your ex-wife has been heavily influenced by the way she was treated by her mother. Her overt beliefs, political, religious, and sexual, may stand in mute testimony to her subtle, subversive beliefs. Her mother did not need to tell her that sex was wrong. She just had to show her that she was uncomfortable whenever the subject was brought up. The mother did not have to sit down and tell her daughter to criticize the husband; she just had to model how to be critical of other people's ideas. Yes, her mother is running your relationship, with minor variation. Look to the dynamics of her family. See how the father is regarded. The grandfather. Watch the body language of the mother towards the father. That is what is in store for you, young man. Unless your ex-wife is one of the rare women that are able to self-reflect and change their views on life-you are in for a full remake of her mother's marriage.

10

THE TRUTH ABOUT
FEMALE HORMONES

Appetizer
Frangelico

Main Course
Guinness Extra Stout

She's in a mood. It's "that time of the month'. PMS. She's pregnant. She's in post-partum depression. She's nursing the baby. She's not nursing the baby. She's having hot flashes. She's going through "the change". These are the common ideas about why women act so irrationally. They are victims of their hormones. It's not their fault. Society gives females every excuse possible to encourage females to give in to their hormonal surges. Does medical science back this claim? What is the real story behind the hormonally-induced moods of women?

One stereotyped view of men portrays them all as creatures at the mercy of our hormones. Balls (or should it be ovaries?) to that, I say. Male hormones undoubtedly have a huge influence on their lives, but there is no reason why men have to become slaves to them. In reality, men are biologically stable creatures when it comes to hormones. The predominant male hormone, testosterone, makes men aggressive, promotes logical thinking, and makes them mentally lust after women most of the day. Testosterone has a very simple, and direct, effect on the behavior of males. They know exactly what they want from minute to minute. They become strong and decisive when the hormones are at their peak. In men it is one predominant hormone with a few different effects. Testosterone tends to keep males functioning at the same moods on a consistent basis. This hormone will decline with age; but it is a gradual decline. Contrary to the popular fantasy among female talk shows hosts, there is no "male menopause" as men mature. A male at 95 years old still produces testosterone, although in lesser amounts than he did at eighteen years old. The same male is still able to obtain an erection (it may take a little while!) and father a child. This steady production enables men to remain rational and composed throughout their lives under a variety of circumstances.

Women, by contrast, tend to fall victim to the rise and fall of different hormones throughout the course of their lives. This daily, monthly, and yearly fluctuation tends to cause the irrational and unpredictable behavior that so characteristically defines human females.

Louann Brizendine's, writer of "The Female Brain" believes that a woman's "neurological reality" is deeply affected by the hormonal surges that fluctuate throughout her life:

"By understanding how hormones affect the female body, mind, and emotions we can understand the hormones negative effects and optimistically try to take advantage of the positive effects."

Most of us, we think, release hormones only after puberty. We cruise along as neutral creatures until we hit puberty and the floodgates of our endocrine system burst open. This is not entirely correct. The fact of the matter is that hormones influence us from the time we are developing fetuses until we die from injuries sustained in a whorehouse fight at 97 years old. It is just that hormones exert different effects at different times in our lives.

The male hormone testosterone makes males aggressive. It also gives them their primary and secondary sex characteristics. The primary sex characteristic is the male appendage. This is what the doctor sees when he says, "It's a boy!" The pecker, wang, schlong, dick, cock, pole, lovestick, tallywhacker, Johnson, rod; and a variety of other names that infest locker rooms and schoolyards across America. The secondary sex characteristics of the male include the Adam's apple, hair on the body, a deep voice, thicker bone structure, increased muscle size and tone, higher levels of thinking, logic, religious philosophy and the ability to form large complex societies with intricate communication networks. Women do not possess testosterone in sufficient quantities to exhibit these traits.

The functionally predominant hormones that influence female primary and secondary sex characteristics are as different and subjective as the various female moods that human males are forced to endure. Estrogen, progesterone, prolactin, estradiol, prostaglandins, oxytocin, and a variety of stimulating hormones such as luteinizing hormone (LH) and follicle stimulating hormone(FSH). Estrogen is responsible for the weak, helpless feeling that seems to run a female human being's life.

When males experience a drop in testosterone production they feel the same weak, helpless feeling. Men with low testosterone feel a loss of sexual desire, a lack of energy, a slowing of hair growth on their body, a nagging feeling to whine about everything, and an inability to make decisions. If it were not for testosterone we would live in a state of perpetual confusion as a society. Testosterone is the hormone that has enabled the human species to live in the advanced technological society that we live in today. But let's not discount the effects of estrogen. Among its other effects, it is also responsible for the growth of breasts. Estrogen's effect on the body is so demonstrative it may cause newborn babies to have slightly enlarged breasts. This usually disappears after a few weeks, but in baby girls mild breast enlargement may reappear sometime in the first two years, this time due to the child's own hormones affecting breast tissue. In other words, babies with excess estrogen will show breast development soon after they are born, but who is going to notice? There have also been documented cases of newborns producing minimal amounts of milk for a week after birth. This breast enlargement may come and go repeatedly over several months, before the hormones level off and disappear throughout later childhood.

At puberty, hormones will begin to alter the female form. Her breasts will grow and take on the shape of an adult woman. She will develop underarm and pubic hair and will get noticeably taller as a significant growth spurt occurs as a result of the influence of estrogen. Much to her chagrin, eventually her menstrual cycle will start. Girls will experience mood changes around this time. Cramps are pretty common during the beginning of the menstrual cycle. This is usually attributed to hormones called prostaglandins. Prostaglandins cause the muscles of the uterus to contract, causing cramps. These cramps usually subside, or lessen, as the girl gets older. From beginning to end, the process of puberty in females usually takes around five years. Some girls experience difficulties adapting to their changing body, budding sexuality, the onset of menses, and emotional instability, as they pass from childhood into adulthood. This is not unusual and may predispose the female for problems in her sexual relationships with males for the rest of her life. Add to this a society that is obsessed with image, lessened brain capacity, various other hormones-and you have the formula for a very confused individual.

All the hormonal components necessary for the onset of puberty are present at birth, but the body keeps it turned off for many years. Eventually, the closed door that prevents puberty opens, and hormones that previously have been held at bay can begin to exert their consequences on the body. A tiny area of the brain called the hypothalamus turns on and starts to release squirts of an assortment of hormones in a periodic manner. This stimulates the pituitary gland (which sits right above the hypothalamus) to produce follicle-stimulating hormone (FSH), and luteinizing hormone (LH), which stimulate a girl's ovaries to produce sex hormones. The two main hormones produced by the ovaries are the female sex hormones, estrogen and progesterone. The ovaries also make a modest amount of the male hormone testosterone. Enough to influence some areas of growth but not enough to really make a difference physically, or intellectually. During puberty, estrogen once again promotes breast development and causes the vagina, uterus, and Fallopian tubes to mature. These are the main parts of the female plumbing system that are involved in pregnancy and parturition (childbirth for those that are not well read). Estrogen also plays a role in the growth spurt of young girls. Another key task of this hormone is to direct the allocation of fat on a girl's body around the hips, butt and thighs. She is slowly becoming her mother in a physical way. The small amounts of testosterone she is manufacturing will promote some muscle and bone growth.

From puberty onwards, FSH, LH, estrogen, estradiol, prolactin, and progesterone all play their individual roles in regulating a woman's menstrual cycle. The cycle is fairly regular, with each individual hormone rising and falling at different stages of the cycle. The 28-day cycle accounts not only for a females moods, but also for the weight gain, water retention, and immensely variable series of psychological and physiological events that have modern science baffled. Women have been driven to commit crimes as heinous as murder during the various phases of the menstrual cycle. One egg (out of several hundred thousand in each ovary) becomes 'ripe' (mature) and is released from the ovary to begin its journey down the Fallopian tube and into the womb. If that egg isn't fertilized, the levels of estrogen and progesterone produced by the ovary begin to fall. Without the supporting action of these hormones, the lining of the womb, which is full of blood, is shed, resulting in a period. Buddy, you are in for it during this time.

Female Hormone Cycle

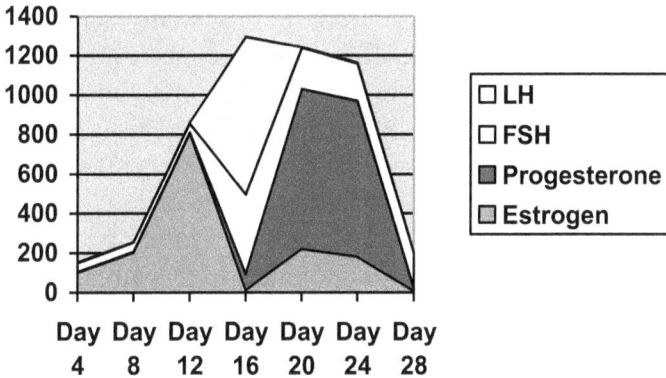

As you can see from the graph the menstrual cycle is a series of peaks and valleys involving the endocrine system. Male humans, or men (as we are more commonly referred to) do not have this wild variation in hormone levels. Without getting too technical, we can see that the level of estrogen peaks around day 12-13. The estrogen level then drastically drops in less than 24 hours. Let us put this in perspective. If this were a testosterone peak and drop, the average male would have run two marathons, lifted weight for six hours straight, fought everyone that looked at him wrong, and then slept like a little baby for a day when the hormone dropped off. But this, thank God, is not testosterone. It is estrogen. The wild fluctuations are responsible for the irrational action of females during the middle of their menstrual cycle. It is also the hormone that makes women horny. If anyone has ever lived with a female for even a month, they know what I am talking about. Yes sir, they know. Maybe we all know that female human beings get horny. It is in every man's interest to understand the hormones which are responsible for the female sexual response; or lack thereof. Women will usually have an increased interest in sexual activity around the time of ovulation. This makes sense. The egg can be fertilized during a relatively short time period. A few days. Nature has selected for those females that increase their sexual activity during this time period. If you are more sexually active when you are ovulating you stand a greater chance of being fertilized. This trait will be passed on to your daughters. In rats, the female will actively pursue the male when she is ovulating. She will move around her cage more, sniff his genitals, and wiggle her ears. These cues tell the male rat that it is time to mate. He hardly argues. We see similar behaviors in human females during ovulation. Go to any nightclub that has dancing. We see men lined up looking for the females that are ovulating. It is rather primitive behavior. However, it is effective. The young lasses that are gyrating on the floor catch the attention of the horny buggers looking from the sides. These voyeuristic men whisper back and forth as to how "hot" she is. Little do they know they are right. If a woman is ovulating her body temperature may increase one degree. She is hot. At least a lot warmer than she was a few days ago. The females on the dance floor that are moving around the most will attract the males the easiest. This rat-like behavior is very similar in most mammals. I don't think that I have ever seen a hot young babe walk up and sniff the genitals of the man she is attracted to. But I don't get around that much to nightclubs either. It may be a new fad one day. It will sure save a lot of time. One sniff and you know she wants it. Sniffing your crotch becomes confirmation that she is interested. A sure sign that you are going to get laid that night.

On a quick aside, females look for the opposite behavior in men on a dance floor. After speaking with hundreds of woman that frequent singles bars I have stumbled upon some new ideas. The guys that dance (like jerks) on the dance floor rarely catch the eye of the female. Females do not want competition. Guys are supposed to look, girls are supposed to dance. The man that moves around the least will attract the most females. The next time you think you are going to get the babes hot by showing your new dance moves- forget it. Let the women do the dancing, you do the looking. Woman have also related that men are even more desirable when they are in groups of five or more. Bring the team the next time you are going out with love on your mind. Single guys are not that attractive to most women in bars. She wants to know that you are not some lone wolf serial killer. I mentioned that female rat's wiggle their ears if they are ovulating. I do not think you will see this behavior in human females. But if you play your cards right you may get to wiggle both her ears later on.

Now back to our hormones. It is the effects of estrogen that make women feel randy. Right before ovulation, the follicles are secreting high amounts of estrogen. High amounts of androgens are also secreted and then converted to estrogen. Androgens are testosterone derived molecules. The androgens convert to estrogen and have an aphrodisiac effect. These androgens may be much stronger in women than men. As the levels of estrogen decrease the level of sexual interest in the female decreases. Consider the case of Bob M. a stockbroker in New York. Bob was a successful trader and had accumulated considerable amounts of money in his 30 years on the planet. Bob M. was involved in a long term relationship with a fine looking young lady from Berkeley, California. Amanda T. was a graduate student at the University of California, Berkeley. She was 24 years old and working on her master's in sociology. They had met in a bar while Bob was in California. Their twice monthly weekends were anything but boring. Here is Bob's story.

When we first met we were obviously attracted to each other. We danced and laughed and fell into the sack that night. We had a great weekend of sex. I had never met a girl that liked to screw as much as I did. When I had to return to New York I thought about her for the whole flight home. When I landed she called me. We have had a long term, monogamous relationship since. However, there are times when she confuses me. She will call me at home on a Tuesday, or Wednesday, and tell me how horny she is. I immediately make a flight for that weekend -, and last minute flights are not cheap. We talk dirty for a few days. By Friday she seems to have slowed down the dirty talk. A few times I would get in waiting for the weekend of sex that I have dreamed about all week – only to be met with a lukewarm attitude to sex. Other times she would be on her period. She would just say that she wanted to cuddle, or go to the museum. There are museums in New York, plenty of them. Anyway, I started noticing a pattern. I am a stockbroker. My success depends on my perception of trends. She would be horny as hell, then nothing. Horny, nothing. I asked a doctor friend of mine if he had heard of similar behavior. He laughed and said, "Yeah, but only from every male patient I have. It's hormonal". I remembered the menstrual cycle from college biology. I laughed at all the PMS jokes at the water cooler over the years. But I never really thought that the female menstrual cycle could have such an impact on her behavior. I made little marks on my calendar- like when she was talking dirty, when she wasn't. I even asked when she was on her period. I felt like I was spying on her. After a couple of months my little science experiment was finished. I had charted her menstrual cycle over a 28 day period. With the help of a few biology books I could tell when she was probably going to ovulate. I could also tell when she was on the rag. Well, call me an asshole, but I now know when to fly to California. I know when I am going to get the most "bang for my buck." I really care about her. I don't want to appear like I want her only for sex. But with my fast-paced schedule I really don't have time to fly to California just to go to a museum. If she is not in a receptive state I just make the flight for the next weekend. I can usually come to within a few days of her "hot time."

Human females go through the same stages of sexual response as do males. Female response is more variable. The stages of sexual response include a general excitement phase, a plateau phase, followed by a resolution phase. In the excitement phase female mammals react to the increased levels of estrogen that are in their body. Some mammals go through seasonal cycles. Like sheep. Sheep are short-day breeders. They breed as the days become shorter. The ewe sends signals to the ram that she is ready for sex. These signals can be auditory, visual, or olfactory. She bleats a lot more. She is making a lot of racket. This is her auditory cue. The ram hears this, stops chewing for a second, and looks her way. Now that he is looking she begins to move around in the field with exaggerated motions. This is her visual cue. The grass drops from the ram's mouth. He begins to walk slowly in her direction. As he gets closer he smells her. She has released chemical messengers in the air. Pheromones. Floating chemicals that attract the male. This is her olfactory cue. The physiological effect of the pheromone is not widely understood. Most mammals send off pheromones to attract a mate. It is the basis of the billion dollar a year perfume industry. Pheromones are what calls all the male cats of the neighborhood to your door when your female cat is in heat. They can smell her for miles. Well the ram is now pretty sure that she wants to mate. All of the signs are there. He walks up, sniffs around a bit, and mounts her. Her excitement phase is over until next year. As is the ram's. She will go through plateau phase and resolution phase. She is ovulating. His sperm will hit their mark and she will become pregnant.

The lamb will develop until the next spring. Giving birth in the spring has advantages for foragers like sheep. There is more food to be eaten. It is warmer. The sheep has developed a strategy that helped it to survive for millennia. The period of receptivity is usually called estrus. Sometimes referred to as being "in heat". In sheep the three phases are very short. Sheep that are engaged in prolonged sexual activity do not look for predators. The ewe gets excited, is mounted, she recovers, and is ready to go again with the next suitor. In less cultured human circles, the word "horny" is used. Very few animals are in heat year round. It takes too much time to be ready to mate every month. The norm for animals is a short breeding season, followed by pregnancy. Childbirth is timed so the young will be born when there is the most food. Two species have strayed from this plan. They also happen to be the two species with the biggest brains- primates and dolphins.

Primates and dolphins are unique in that they breed year round. Humans and dolphins seem to be the only animals that have sex for fun. The females of both the species can get pregnant on a monthly basis. They are receptive to the male at any time during the menstrual cycle (as anyone that has earned his "Redwings" knows!) The three phases in humans are affected by different hormones. The period of time associated with development of the follicle and ovulation is referred to as the estrous cycle. The estrous cycle is analogous to the menstrual cycle of the human female. However, most animals (non-primates) will only mate during specific parts of the estrous cycle. Estrous refers to the entire ovarian cycle in the female. Depending on the species this cycle varies greatly. Rats cycle every 4 or 5 days. Humans every thirty days. It is during the various stages of estrous that the female shows receptivity in most creatures. Most animals will not show mating behavior when the female is not in a period of estrous. The female will fight off the male. Internally there will be no receptivity even if the male advances. The male will usually not approach the female unless she is displaying copulatory behaviors specific to that species. Humans are not that much different. Most sexual behaviors are characterized by three stages, attractivity, proceptivity, and receptivity.

Attractivity is measured by the amount of time a male will spend in the vicinity of the female. Some factors may enhance attraction. The male is attracted more to the female when her estrogen levels are the highest. This may indicate a pheromone attractant. A chemical signal that is given off by the female and travels through the air into the male olfactory system. Once in the male this hormone will stimulate him to ready himself for a sexual encounter. Flirting behaviors during this time increase a male's attraction to a female.

Proceptivity is the degree to which the female initiates the sex act, or copulation. This can be measured by what the female will do to obtain a mate and have sex with him. Proceptivity can be determined by the attractiveness of the male to the female. It can also be determined by the levels of testosterone in the female's circulatory system at this time. In the complex world of human sexual response there are countless mitigating factors that will determine proceptivity. From handcuffs to soft music, each female will be stimulated by a different set of circumstances to become proceptive.

Receptivity is the state of responsiveness to the sexual initiation of the male. A kiss, a light brush across her nipples, or the appearance of the rest of the softball team, will all make females react differently during the receptive phase of her sexual 'attractivity'.

Let's talk a little about progesterone. This is the "feel good" hormone. This is the hormone that makes a female want to prepare her nest. This is the hormone that makes women want to cuddle. This is only a few short days after she has accused you of having an affair, thinking she is fat, looking at other women, blaming you for her non-orgasmic state, and telling you that your mother screwed you up from childhood! Now she wants to cuddle! And what does she blame her previous day's behavior on? Why, PMS of course. So let's have a look at PMS.

Scientists still don't know whether hormones are responsible for the wide range of physical and psychological symptoms we now call premenstrual syndrome or PMS. No-one doubts that many women experience tender breasts, abdominal bloating, irritability, poor mood and other symptoms in the days before their period. Whether these are due to hormone fluctuations, changes in brain chemicals, social and emotional problems or a combination of all three is a matter of debate.

"I'm bloated."
"You think I'm getting fat."
"I'm just , ooh, irritable."
"I DON'T KNOW WHY–YOU'RE JUST AN ASS-HOLE!"
"I want out of this relationship."
"I love you so much." (minutes later) *"I fucking hate you!"*

These are just a few of the common statements that women experiencing PMS symptoms will say. Now these allegedly nurturing, stable, maternal, creatures which are fully in touch with their feelings are striking out- at you. This is a documented condition and fully accepted by the medical establishment. The hormonal swings that we spoke of earlier (see the graph) are entirely responsible for the otherwise sedate, loving female in question's behavior. So at least once a month a woman is entitled, almost encouraged, to acting totally insane and not taking responsibility for her actions. It is as if it comes out of nowhere, and then leaves just as fast a few days later. And buddy, you had better shut up about it if you want to enjoy at least a portion of the rest of the three weeks before the next episode.

PMS has been implicated in many crimes that women have committed. There have been a few studies that seem to corroborate that PMS cause a women to allow her hormones to cloud her judgment. There was a case of a prominent female surgeon that used PMS as her defense in a drunk driving case. This female surgeon (femsurgeon?) was stopped by a state trooper one Thanksgiving night. The trooper noticed a strong odor of alcohol on the breath of the woman, who was driving her children home from a dinner party. When asked how much she had to drink the femsurgeon became irate and told the trooper that she was a doctor and that it was "none of his damn business" how much she had to drink that night. When asked to put her hands on the top of her head she tried to kick him in the groin. According to the report she then screamed at the officer:

"You son of a bitch; you can't do this to me - I'm a doctor. I hope you get shot and come into my hospital so I can refuse to treat you, or if any other trooper gets shot, I will refuse to treat them!"

After being arrested the doctor was asked to take the Breathalyzer test, whereupon she kicked the sensitive instrument. When finally she took the test, she failed with a blood alcohol well over the legal limit. She was charged with drunk driving. Cut and dried? Not quite, Sparky. This incident happened in the enlightened liberal state of Virginia. The wonderful doctor pleaded that she was heavily afflicted with premenstrual syndrome. Her lawyer argued that women during this time will absorb alcohol quicker than the average person, and that the hostility was a result of the hormones that were surging through the alcohol-laced blood of this maniac! And guess what? She was acquitted!

Yessirree, Bob. She was let go. Let go to do what? To practice intricate, delicate surgery. Yes, surgery that requires patience, a cool head under stress, and calm logical decision-making based any anything but emotions. Should the patients be forewarned? Should the surgeon be made to show where she is on her monthly menstrual cycle before she comes in to the surgery ward? Light surgery on days 12-14, brain surgery on any other day? This same defense has been used successfully many times, even in murder trials.

> *"It wasn't her fault your honor, she was PMSing"*
> *"Well, I guess we can overlook it this time if she tells us where she buried the bodies."*

Could you imagine if a male human being tried to use hormones as a defense in a murder trial? He would be laughed out of court right into the prison showers.

But wait, there was a case of a male using bad hormones as a defense. Remember Richard Speck? He killed eight nurses in a single night in June of 1966. Speck tried to use the defense that he was a "Supermale". That is, he had an extra "Y" chromosome. He produced too much male hormone. Testosterone. The hormone responsible for a man's sex drive and male aggressiveness. Whereas the normal male has an XY chromosome, some males are born with an extra "Y" chromosome. It is the "Y" chromosome that genetically determines whether one is a male or female. It is alleged that the extra "Y"chromosome would make one a "Supermale", super-aggressive, and super-horny. His aggressiveness, because of this genetic addition, was fueled by his overwhelming libido. Testosterone made him a sex-crazed killer. He killed eight innocent human beings. The hormone defense did not hold for Speck and the nasty bugger was sentenced to death. His sentence was later commuted to life when the state abolished the death penalty. Maybe he should have tried the PMS defense. Drink your beer.

Ω

Pregnancy. If the egg released from the ovary is fertilized and a pregnancy results, a woman's fluctuating hormones change again. This is the beginning of the end of your sex life. As stated in a previous chapter, from this point forward she will be taking her cues from her mother. Her mother's behavior is now the only guide that she can use to navigate through the unknown waters ahead. She sure as hell isn't going to ask you! But that is not the whole story. The real truth goes beyond her childhood training. It is biology at its best. Best for the child, not your soon to be neglected pecker. The magnanimous changes that are taking place are incomprehensible to the steady thought pattern of the average male human. But woman know what is going on. Have you ever seen two women that are pregnant? They do not even have to know each other, but they are already bonded. It is as if they are aliens from the planet Preggo. They have a secret code that only they can read.

Here is what is happening hormonally. The usual drop in estrogen and progesterone at the end of the menstrual cycle fails to occur, so there is no menstrual flow. The average male is usually ecstatic at this, but the tide quickly changes. Men begin to beg for the old menstrual flow after the hormones of pregnancy take center stage. You thought once a month was bad? Hold on, pardner, this is going to be a bumpy ride! A new hormone, HCG (human chorionic gonadotrophin), primed by our little love zygote, push the ovaries to pump higher levels of estrogen and progesterone into her bloodstream. Her moods are changing once again. She has cravings. Morning sex is being replaced by morning sickness. This is due to the sudden increase in hormones in her body. These higher levels are needed to keep a pregnancy going. Pregnancy testing kits are designed to detect HCG in a woman's urine, and pick up even trace amounts even a day or so after her first missed period. And it's going to get better.

Now there are two ways to look at this. One is that you are going to produce a beautiful child, made out of the love that you shared with this wonderful woman. Childbirth is a miracle. From the day you see your baby come blinking into the world, to the day your child has their own child, your life is full of wonder and awe. Another way to look at this is that you have gone from master cocksman, Tarzan of the Penis World, to a blue-balled cuckold whose only purpose is to provide food and shelter. Maybe if you are lucky you can carry the baby in a man sling baby back-pack, or push the stroller while your wife shops for baby clothes.

It is at this point that you begin to realize what sex is all about. But, yet, you hold out hope. Your tallywacker is depending on you. "He" is still being coerced by his myopic, single hormone. He is confused as to the sudden turn of events. He asks you, *"What have I done wrong?"* or for the religious, *"Oh, God, why have you forsaken me?"* in rigid protest. He is going to show you, night and day, that he is ready for action. In the middle of a board meeting, just like in high school, he stands up for attention. No response? Wait till tonight. You can sleep, but you can't hide. "He" is there in the morning ready for her to blow reveille, and stands alone. She is in the bathroom, either peeing or puking. Your ear cannot discern the difference now. All that matters is that you are alone, in a bed, with a hard-on. Isn't this how you started? Is this not why you wanted to get married in the first place? Of course, we wanted love and a family.

But deep down, it was really Mr. Schlongmeister that had us convinced that we were going to be happy. Yes, it was Mr. Schlongmeister that picked this one out in the first place. The tits, the ass, the garter belts, the dirty talk, ummm. And then you find your hand choking Mr. Schlongmeister. Is it the choke of manual five-digit love? Or is it the choke of: *"You asshole, you got me into this situation!"* Either way, you and Mr. Schlongmeister are no longer on speaking terms. For awhile, at least. You already know that "He" is weak. "He" will be the first one to break the ice, to reach out (literally). "He" will turn your head to look at the girl walking down the street in the tight red miniskirt. "He" will make you wonder if she is wearing panties under that tight... skintight... almost caressing...her ass... sliding up and down with every step she takes...oh, please, wind, blow it up...and he will not stop until you talk to him. You may have seen a man in this predicament. Walking down the street, a pretty girl walks by scantily clad, and he smiles saying out loud (to his penis), *"Oh no, that is not for us, we're married with a pregnant wife."* and then the smile quickly fades because he know that he has once again disappointed his best "friend". But the fun isn't over yet, is it?

In the fourth month of pregnancy, the love zygote, also called the placenta, overtakes the ovaries as the main producer of estrogen and progesterone. These hormones have a few effects. They cause the lining of the womb to thicken, which is exactly what every man wants. These two evil hormones increase the volume of blood circulating to the love zygote and now tender, off-limits breasts. They also loosen the muscles of the pelvis, uterus, and vagina to make room for the your little baby. (Remember the word, "loosen"; you will hear it again later in this chapter.)

After the fourth month the baby is usually fully developed. The female body has become accustomed to the foreign being growing inside. Aside from some minor hormonal changes, this will be the time that the physiological part of the pregnancy has leveled off. Most of what takes place in the remaining months is growth of the baby. She is "eating for two". She is getting fat. Her breasts are the biggest they have ever been in her life. They look good, but on a basal level you know they are no longer yours. They have a purpose beyond your immature squeezing and nipple licking. They are being filled with milk for the baby. They are for the baby. They are no longer yours. And they will never be the same. The nipples get darker and bigger. They are not as sensitive. You will never kiss them the same. You will never squeeze them with such vigor again. They have been tainted. They have evolved. You are still living in the past while these breasts are fulfilling the purpose for which they were designed. Feeding the mammalian offspring of a human being. Years after the "baby" has graduated from college you will still feel that these tits have betrayed you. They left you and came back worn out and demoralized. Nature won. It used you to produce a viable offspring while you stared at tits. It was a Darwinian example of "bait and switch". See these tits? Aren't they nice? Keep coming closer…closer…and BAM! They are gone and you are left watching the girls in the mall while your wife shops for baby clothes. Sitting with the rest of the fathers, holding the bags, waiting for what used to be your girlfriend to leave the baby clothes store. You muster up a feigned look of excitement when you see the clothes that she has picked out for the baby. The words, *"aren't those cute"* leave your lips before you can stop yourself. All because of a pair of tits. Nice tits. Tits that are still there, but yet they are not there. You see young men walking with their girlfriends in the mall. You want to scream out, *"RUN! THEY KEEP THE TITS AFTER YOU PAY FOR THEM!"* But you know it is in vain. Like a prisoner on the way to Auschwitz, you will only draw the ire of the guards if you protest. Once inside the Secret World of Lost Tits, you will never be allowed to leave. You cannot tell your secret to anyone. For even if you did, no one would believe you. You could no sooner convince that horny nineteen-year-old boy that his girl- friend breasts are a decoy, than you would have been convinced at that age. All is lost. The tits have won. You are another casualty of The Great Tit Conspiracy.

Ω

So you sit quietly in the mall, surrounded by stores that cater to women. Clothing stores, baby stores, kids' clothing stores, pregnancy stores, fat broad stores, and shoe stores with 99% of their inventory full of women's shoes. You feel a wave of energy as you say to the tit-duped, bag-laden "man" sitting next to you, *"Did you ever notice that there are no men's stores in this mall?"*

To which he dully replies, *"Well there's the tool department in Sears, and the, uh...food court."*

To which you grimace in acknowledgement. Like a concentration camp prisoner, you try to look at the bright side as you watch the young men being led through the mall on the path to despair by a beautiful girl with a lovely set of tits. You pick up your bags and follow your wife to the next store like a good husband. You begin to notice she is waddling. A tear forms at the corner of your eye. You convince yourself that it is a tear of joy at how happy you are with your new role in life. You convince yourself that your wife is even more beautiful when she's pregnant. You begin to wonder if the terrorist ever considered crashing a plane into a mall. But you know that they know that malls are the emotional torture chambers of the Americas. They wouldn't want to end that. You smile with everything you can as your wife tells you to hurry up. The next 5 months will be the worst of your life as the reality of your situation sinks in.

Ω

Around the time of childbirth, other hormones attack the female body that help the uterus to contract during labor. One of these is called oxytocin. Oxytocin also stimulates the breast to produce and release human milk. Childbirth is a very emotionally and physically draining experience. After childbirth, what then? Levels of estrogen, progesterone and other hormones fall sharply, causing a number of physical changes. The womb shrinks back to its non-pregnant size, pelvic floor muscle tone improves and the volume of blood circulating round the body returns to normal. The dramatic changes in hormone levels might also play a part in causing postnatal depression, although no real differences have been found in the hormone changes of women who do, and do not, get postnatal depression. It may be that some women are more easily affected by these hormonal fluctuations than others.

As Jim Morrison so eloquently put it, *"This is the end, the end, my friend, the end."* He may not have been singing about menopause but he may as well have been. The next significant hormonal change for most women occurs around the time of the last period - the menopause. Over three to five years leading up to a woman's last period, the normal functioning of her ovaries begins to deteriorate. This can cause her menstrual cycle to become shorter or longer, and sometimes it becomes quite erratic. Periods may become heavier or lighter. Eventually, the ovaries produce so little estrogen that the lining of the womb fails to thicken up and so periods stop altogether.

For most of a woman's life, estrogen helps to protect the heart and bones, as well as maintaining the breasts, womb, vagina and bladder in their healthy state. The marked loss of estrogen in a woman's body that occurs around, and after, the menopause can, therefore, have detrimental effects on her health; as well as causing uncomfortable symptoms such as hot flushes and night sweats, lack of estrogen can increase the risk of heart disease and the bone disorder osteoporosis. Other problems include vaginal dryness, discomfort during sex, recurrent urine infections and incontinence. It may also contribute to the depression, irritability and poor concentration, which some menopausal women experience. But menopause doesn't have to be a disastrous time for women - if reduced hormone levels do cause unpleasant symptoms, treatments such as hormone replacement therapy (HRT) are often very effective. HRT and other types of medication can also be used to prevent health problems, for example if a woman has a significantly increased risk of developing osteoporosis or heart disease in the future.

So, from the cradle to the grave, hormones play an important role in every woman's life. They shape their bodies (quite literally) as well as some of the most important events they experience, from pregnancy and childbirth to the menopause. There may be times when you curse your body's hormones, but console yourself with the thought that life without them would be much less interesting!

11

Appetizer
Wild Turkey

Main Course
Dos Equis XX

ADVICE ON HOW TO SURVIVE
YOUR DIVORCE

We have discussed various theories throughout this book. Some have merit, others need more research. That is the way of science. There are many fantastic, well-adjusted women out there, but, due to their rarity, the average American male will probably never find one. This book has, hopefully, made light of some of the common situations that men find themselves trapped in (concerning women). There are ways to survive your divorce. And maybe, just maybe, not only survive - but to actually enjoy the company of a woman; and have a deep, meaningful relationship. Perhaps we will eternally ponder the question posed by Professor Henry Higgins in the 1964 Tony Award winning musical, *My Fair Lady*,

"Why can't a woman be more like a man?"

Higgins elaborates further,

> *"Women are irrational, that's all there is to that! Their heads are full of cotton, hay, and rags. They're nothing but exasperating,*

irritating, vacillating, calculating, agitating, maddening and infuriating hags!"

An excellent, well-respected play and movie with a good bit of insight into the female mind. So how does the average man in Mammerica deal with the irrational behavior of the average female? A few tidbits of advice that may help manage your anger as she attempts to interrupt your dreams, scrape your soul from your body, and pick you to death.

Ω

The foremost idea is that you cannot make a woman happy. If you work hard to make money to buy her nice things and provide her with a beautiful house in the suburbs, she complains that you're never home, you are distant and never pay attention to her. If you quit that job for a less demanding one and spend time with her she will say that you are always underfoot and never give her any space, or that you do not make enough money. If you want to have sex with her frequently she will rebuff you as using her for sex. If you do not have sex with her frequently she will rebuff you for your low sex drive -and tell all of her friends about it; as a matter of fact, she will tell her friends about everything you do (as we discussed in a previous chapter). If you spend time with the children she will say you are not spending time with her. If you spend time with her she will say you are neglecting the children. Take her out a lot and she complains about spending too much money. Don't take her out and she complains that you never go out. Spend time with the boys and she complains about that. Stay home to be with her and she says that you are "up her ass" every night. Not literally of course, because then she would complain about that. If you have a sexual fetish she will find fault with it. If you do not have a sexual fetish she will say that you are boring in bed. If you don't tell her she is beautiful – stand by. If you do tell her she is beautiful she will ignore the compliment – or accuse you of just trying to get laid. Once the male of the relationship realizes that he cannot make his female happy he will have arrived at enlightenment. The man cannot win, so why try?

The female human being, through evolution, and social conditioning, has been trained to never be happy. That is especially true of American women. Women in other cultures will have a degree of peace that American women do not possess. With American women it is constant derision of their men that seems to make them function.

Men squander thousands of dollars, millions even, trying to buy women expensive gifts to make them happy. It rarely works. The richest female (that may have only a high school degree) married to a wealthy man that lavishes her with trips to Europe and expensive jewelry is as predictably unhappy with her husband as is the college graduate that married a lower middle-class working stiff. Women are gloomy, dismal creatures. When a man accepts that he is neither responsible for a women's happiness, nor her unhappiness, he will be able to move on with his life to find serenity and fulfillment. If a man spends his life trying to please his woman, he will simply throw away his life trying to please his woman. Very seldom will he succeed. The unhappiness of the average Mammerican woman is punctuated with one thing. Drama.

If a man has decided that he has had enough and gives up on his wife, she will then activate her "female scorned genes". Extreme anger, or increased attention to him, will become the new behavior. The only thing women cannot stand more than being liked-is being disliked. Because they do not like themselves. It is the man that realizes this sad fact that will be able to best tolerate the psychotic behavior that women exhibit.

In their lives, in their literature, in their movies, and their television shows-women live for drama. Their minds cannot handle heavy intellectual processes like, uh, say building a civilization. This is left up to the man. Their minds love conflict and misery. When a man and a woman have a disagreement the man will think clearly and rationally for a quick solution. Consider the situation: two men are at odds in a bar. Both men will strut and puff up their chest in the hopes that the other will quickly back down. If neither backs down – a fist fight will ensue. At the conclusion of the fight the problem has been resolved and both men can go on with their lives amid high intellectual thought. When two women are at odds the fight never happens. The opposing females love the drama so much they will drag it out for hours, even weeks. They involve all of their friends, their friends' friends, and anyone else that will listen. Their minds need to be occupied and drama occupies the female mind more than any other thought. Men go insane trying to solve a women's problems because they do not get what women really want. Women want their problems to shade out reality. They want commotion in their lives to keep their minds engaged. Otherwise they will have to watch drama, read drama, or hear about someone else's drama. Secondhand drama works for awhile, but most women like their own drama. Understand this- and you will have half the battle won.

The blockbuster hit, *'I Am Legend'*, starring Will Smith, epitomizes what women are all about. When Will's character, Robert Neville, is trying to save the world, all his wife can think about is herself. She wants him to abandon his quest to save all of mankind from this worldwide plague just to comfort her as she leaves the hot zone in a helicopter. No plan, no care for humanity, no thought of anyone but herself. Take care of me! How many times have you seen that in the movies? The accurate portrayal of women adds to the realism of any film. It is the female that is always trying to get our hero to abandon his cause just to take care of her and make her feel safe. In the film, *'JFK'*, Jim Garrison (Kevin Costner) is trying to bring to justice the conspirators in the greatest crime of the twentieth century-the Kennedy assassination. His wife is more concerned with going to the relatives for Sunday dinner than bringing the assassins to justice. Sound familiar?

Furthermore, cast off the hope that women will ever communicate like men. There is about as much chance as that happening as there is a blind three-legged dairy cow playing violin for the Boston Pops. It is close to impossible. Women communicate differently because their entire brain is wired differently than a man's brain. There are those rare birds that were exposed to the miracle hormone testosterone in the womb, and then raised with brothers, and grew up to be good-looking and personable. Let me know when you find one like this that is not doing porn movies or dancing on a stage in West Palm Beach. These women are great finds. Especially if they let you fall in love with them. To quote Henry David Thoreau, *"Most men lead lives of quiet desperation and go to the grave with the song still in them."* Could it be because the mass of women are irrational, confused, angry individuals and this causes the mass of men to lead lives of quiet desperation? Ponder the connection. The men that fell for the false advertising of hot monogamy before the marriage paid daily for the rest of their life. Women will always communicate like women. That is their evolutionary niche. And evolutionarily the strategy is working; humans are more numerous now than at any time in our biological history. Women do not need to know how to communicate to men. They must know how to attract a man and get him to support her and her children-by hook or by crook. They have to be ahead of the other women. It is essential for women to be able to compete and outmaneuver other women for their very survival as a desirable, reproductive mammal. There is no requirement for a woman to evolve a complex set of communication skills to deal with men. Nature gave women sexuality. They use this to deal with men in a very effective manner. So the "60's girl" was no more socially evolved than the "80's girl". The "21st Century" girl will still be as intellectually limited as women were during the Victorian era. Women do not communicate well and they surely do no communicate their feelings to men well. Mainly because women do not understand men. Women cannot understand men because they lack the gray matter to do so. Period.

Ω

Women do not listen to what the man is saying; she is listening to how he is saying it. That is why women do not succeed in fields that require quick decisions. She cannot separate the deed from the doer. If a woman were President of the United States, she would not like certain countries because of their tone, or their attitude, or "just because". If a woman were President, we would live on the brink of nuclear annihilation as her hormones fluctuated each month. Women are fundamental creatures of nature. They were designed to perpetuate the species. Men are creatures of progress- physically, intellectually and spiritually. They were designed to propel the human race to the stars and beyond. That is the major difference between the sexes.

When an alcoholic finally admits that his drinking is beyond his control he contemplates the Twelve Steps made legendary by Alcoholics Anonymous. Let us consider the Twelve Steps towards surviving our female significant others' in the 21st century.

The Twelve Steps of Coping with Your Divorce

1. I will admit that I am powerless over female irrationality. Attempting to reason with females is meaningless and has left me bitter, confused, and lonely.

2. I believe that a Power greater than me can restore me to sanity.

3. I will make a decision to blame God for the shortcomings of women. I will turn my life over to the care of God, as I understand Him. He must have a good reason for allowing women to behave so irrationally.

4. I will make a searching and fearless moral inventory of myself, and will most likely find out that –" it ain't me, it's her."

5. I will admit to God, to myself, and to other men the exact nature of my wrongs in trying to communicate with women.

6. I forgive my ex-wife for pointing out my physical and personal defects while I was married to her and thank goodness that I do not have to hear it anymore.

7. I will humbly ask my ex-wife to relate to her girlfriends my shortcomings as often as possible. (Why not, she's going to do it anyway!)

8. I will make a list of all of the people that I have harmed in my futile quest to understand female behavior; and I am prepared to make amends to them.

9. I will make direct amends to such people wherever possible, except when to do so would be impossible, or if it would just give her something else to complain about and file for more alimony.

10. I will continue to take personal inventory, and whether I am right or wrong, promptly admit that I am wrong. It is the only way to shut her up.

11. I will seek, through prayer and meditation, to improve my conscious contact with God, as I understand Him, praying only for knowledge of His will for me and the power to put up with my ex-wife for as long as I did.

12. Having had a spiritual awakening as the result of these steps, I will try to carry this message to other men stuck in miserable relationships (oxymoron?), and to practice these principles in all my affairs.

Those twelve steps may help. Realize also that women cannot be happy. There are too many factors affecting their mind for it to free itself and seek true happiness.

Therefore, what do you, as a male, do to squeeze at least a little of your overly idealized happiness out of your marriage? Treat your significant other as you would a child. You would not get upset at your three-year-old nephew if he did not understand how to rebuild your 1950 Corvette engine, would you? Anymore than you would get upset at the neighbors' son for not understanding what you are saying about satellite transmissions in the early 1950's. Women do not understand the higher thought processes of men. This is evidenced by the huge gap in communication that men and women possess. Men get frustrated with women because they want women to be more comprehensive of their meanings. Like men. They desperately want woman to be rational. They want to be friends with women, to be able to count on them. Some loyalty would be nice. They see women as sexual creatures and think what they, with their male brain, would do if they had a nice ass and full, supple breasts. They get astounded when they realize that women cannot function at the abstract and theoretical level of thinking that men possess. Maybe men should cope with women, as one would deal with a child that does not understand a subject. Speak softly, slowly. Moreover, have a lot of patience. Realize that she is probably not listening to the content of what you say, but the feel of it. She is looking for that feeling that is going to affect her as a woman. This is how nature made her.

The basic differences between a man and a woman are contradictory in almost all situational interactions. Men speak to offer information or testimony. Women talk to gather information or solicit empathy. Men seek order, rules and organization. Women rebel against order, rules and organization. Men are focused, detailed, and logical. Women are scattered, broad and irrational. Men are assertive. Women seek consensus. Men talk about events and ideas. Women talk about people. Men flourish on competition and accomplishment. Women thrive on feeling good and acceptance. Men concentrate on facts, deduction, and logic. Women concentrate on feelings, senses and meaning. Men seek intellectual understanding. Women seek sympathy. Men find answers by examination and evaluation. Women find answers by intuition. But men want to think. Women want to feel. The basic differences of men and women would be enough to make them two different species. But they are not. The human being that you are in a relationship with is the same species, cruelly selected for by nature to reproduce and ensure that her offspring live to reproduce at any cost. Relationships between men and woman are paradoxical by nature. Very few escape the strong hand of Mother Nature.

Ω

But remember – while *his* ancestors built civilizations, *her* ancestors were picking berries.

Epilogue

Dessert
Dom Perignon

This book does not paint women in a favorable pose. It almost makes one think that men do not need women. We do. For all of their frustrating, irrational behavior women are still very satisfying to be around. They are fun to date, exciting to work with, awesome to look at, and stimulating to touch. Without women, men most likely would not have done anything except sit in the cave and watch cave football. How would we ever know? Biblically, God saw that Adam was, well, incomplete. So he made him a "help-meet" to help meet his needs. Maybe the exasperating things that women do have a purpose, I mean look at what we do for them- we fight wars, sing songs, lay our coats over puddles, spend exorbitant amounts of money on wining and dining, buy expensive diamond rings, and turn our back on our best friend if he does her wrong. Their irrationality intrigues us. Their frailty vitalizes us. Their bodies excite us. Other men can be friends to us. Great friends, even lifelong friends. We lay down our lives for other men and their ideas. But nothing gets into our head like a women does. Her smell, her eyes, her silky hair. Ahh, they are a royal nuisance but none of us can go a day without thinking about one.

Think of a world full of one sex. Aside from gay men, the majority of us would have no incentive. Why did you want to be the football star in high school? Women. Why do you want to make money? To spend on women. To impress women. To get women to like you. To be around women. If we had only one sex would we even fight any wars? There would be nothing to fight over. Oh, you want to live on my land? Go ahead, I will move over here - it is a big planet. There would be no reason to fight. No one to amaze. Without women this would be one boring planet.

So does that mean women are only here for our entertainment and companionship? That is a discussion that will never end. And maybe they are. Who am I to say? I have met some great women in my life. Having been in education for most of my adult life I can honestly say that two out of the three best principals I have ever worked for were women. They were just, well, better. More organized, more empathic, better at the curriculum, and outstanding at evaluating what teachers need to improve. Both principals are still working in the education field. One is principal of a high school in West Palm Beach (her sister was a Playboy centerfold), and the other is the greatest principal I have ever had the privilege of working with. She is currently a principal in a middle school south of Charlotte, North Carolina. This book is intended to be a catharsis for men that have had difficulty with women. I almost did not write the book in the slim chance I would offend the greatest principal I have ever met. But I think she will understand. Women are indispensable and we know it. I hope this manuscript has enlightened us as to the differences between men and women so that we stop trying to change each other.

Viva la difference.

Bibliography

Reuwen Achiron, Shlomo Lipitz, & Anat Achiron. *Sex-related differences in the development of the human fetal corpus callosum: in utero ultrasonographic study. Prenatal Diagnosis, 2001, 21:116-120.*

M. de Lacoste, R. Holloway, and D. Woodward. *Sex differences in the fetal human corpus callosum, Human Neurobiology, 1986, 5(2):93-6.*

Christine Mack, Robert McGivern, Lynn Hyde, & Victor Denenberg. *Absence of postnatal testosterone fails to demasculinize the male rat's corpus callosum. Developmental Brain Research, 1996, 95:252-254.*

Tracey J. Shores & George Miesegaes. *Testosterone in utero and at birth dictates how stressful experience will affect learning in adulthood. Proceedings of the National Academy of Sciences, 99:13955-13960, October 15, 2002.*

Gwendolyn Wood & Tracey J. Shors. *Stress facilitates classical conditioning in males, but impairs classical conditioning in females through activational effects of ovarian hormones. Proceedings of the National Academy of Sciences, 95:4066-4071, 1998.*

Caplan, Paula, PhD. *They Say you're Crazy, 1995,* Perseus Books.

Bertram, B. *Social factors influencing reproduction in wild lions. Journal of Zoology, London, 1975. 177: p. 463-482.*

Bygott, D., Bertram, B., & Hanby, J. *Male lions in large coalitions gain reproductive advantages. Nature, 1979. 282(20): p. 839-841.*

Grinnell, J., Packer, C., & Pusey, A. *Cooperation in male lions: kinship, reciprocity or mutualism? Animal Behavior, 1995. 49(1): p. 95-105.*

Grinnell, J.M., Karen. *Maternal grouping as a defense against infanticide by males: evidence from field playback experiments on African lions. Behavioral Ecology, 1996. 7(1): p. 55-59.*

Heinsohn, R.P., Craig. *Complex Cooperative Strategies in Group-Territorial African Lions. Science, 1995. 269(5228): p. 1260-1262.*

Packer, C.P., Anne. *Adaptations of Female Lions to Infanticide by Incoming Males. The American Naturalist, 1983. 121(5): p. 716-728.*

Packer, C.P., Anne. *Intrasexual Cooperation and the Sex Ratio in African Lions. The American Naturalist, 1987. 130(4): p. 636-642.*

Packer, S., & Pusey. *Why Lions Form Groups: Food Is Not Enough. The American Naturalist, 1990. 136(1): p. 1-19.*

Packer, C.P., Anne. *The Lack Clutch in a Communal Breeder: Lion Litter Size is a Mixed Evolutionarily Stable Strategy. The American Naturalist, 1995. 145(5): p. 833-841.*

Packer, C.H., Robert. *Lioness Leadership. Science, 1996. 271(5253): p. 1215-1216.*

Packer, C., Pusey, A. E., & Eberly, L. *Egalitarianism in Female African Lions. Science, 2001. 293(5530): p. 690-693.*

Roach, J. Female Lions Are Democratic in Breeding, Study Finds. 2001, National Geographic News. <http://news.nationalgeographic.com/news/2001/07/0726_1 ionequality.html>.

Spong, G. *Space use in lions, Panthera leo, in the Selous Game Reserve: social and ecological factors. Behavioral Ecology & Sociobiology, 2002. 52: p. 303-307.*

Trivedi, B.P. *Female Lions Prefer Dark-Maned Males, Study Finds. 2002, National Geographic News. <http://news.nationalgeographic.com/news/2002/08/0822_ 020822_TVlion.html>.*

West, P.P., Craig. *Sexual Selection, Temperature, and the Lion's Mane. Science, 2002. 297(5585): p. 1339-1343.*

Wallerstein JS, Lewis JM, Blakeslee S. *The unexpected legacy of divorce: a twenty-five year landmark study. New York: Hyperion; 2000.*

Felitti VJ, Anda RF, Nordenberg D, et al. *Relationship of childhood abuse and household dysfunction to many of the leading causes of death in adults. The Adverse Childhood Experiences (ACE) Study. Am J Prev Med 1998 May;14(4):245-58.*

Look for more exciting work from this author and A-Argus
Better Book Publishers

www.ingramcontent.com/pod-product-compliance
Lightning Source LLC
Chambersburg PA
CBHW071418090426
42737CB00011B/1503